THE
BIBLE
PARENTING CODE

THE BIBLE

PARENTING CODE

Revealing God's Perfect Parenting Plan

JOHN ROSEMOND

Carpenter's Son Publishing

Published by Carpenter's Son Publishing, Franklin, Tennessee

Published in association with Larry Carpenter of Christian Book Services, LLC

www.christianbookservices.com

Interior Layout Design by Adept Content Solutions

Printed in the United States of America

978-1-952025-69-3

ACKNOWLEDGMENTS

I owe sincere thanks to:

Willie, for accepting that writing a book requires long hours. I cannot imagine spending my life with anyone else. Who else would accept that I'd rather be a rock star?

Scott Gleason, my pastor at Tabernacle Baptist Church, who is about the wittiest man I've ever known. If I am in some ways deserving of some form of medieval "correction," he won't tell anyone.

Lynn and Steve Stroud, Marilyn and Emmett Reynolds, Nola and Jay Livingston, Anne and Jim Schout, and Stacey Watts for reading portions of this book as I was writing it and providing valuable feedback. You guys are a Godsend, truly. Willie and I are blessed to know you and call you friends!

John Howard, faithful agent and faithful friend. You, too, Chrys!

Larry Carpenter, Shane Crabtree, and all the good folks at Christian Publishing Services in Franklin, Tennessee, for believing in my work.

The psychology licensing boards of North Carolina and Kentucky for making my life difficult and, in so doing, causing me to become a whole lot smarter and well-informed.

The parents of America and around the world who have put trust in my advice. You have caused me to understand what humility is truly all about.

Christ Jesus, for opening the door when I knocked, not quite sure what I would find. It is inexpressibly wonderful to be one of your kids.

CONTENTS

Preface ix

Introduction xiii

1. History Repeats Itself (Gen. 11:5–7) 1
2. In The Beginning (Gen. 2:24) 7
3. Fool's Gold (Col. 2:8) 15
4. Foundations (Ps. 11:3) 19
5. Worldview (Col. 2:20–23) 27
6. Parents As God's "Imagers" (Gen. 1:26–27) 31
7. Awards Mean Nada To God (Deut. 6:6–7) 37
8. The Seasons Of Parenthood (Eccles. 3:1) 41
9. The First Parenting Commandment (Matt. 22:35–39) 49
10. The Second Parenting Commandment (Matt. 22:40) 53
11. Parent With Vision! (Prov. 22:6) 57
12. The Congenital State Of The Heart (Prov. 22:15) 65
13. The Rod (Prov. 22:15) 69
14. Alpha Speech (Matt. 5:37) 73
15. A Mutuality Of Exasperation (Eph. 6:4) 77
16. The Holy Purpose Of Tradition (Ex. 20:12) 85
17. Grandma Was Right After All! (Eccles. 1:9) 91
18. Fly High, Fall Hard (Matt. 23:12) 95
19. The Blessings Of Fear (Prov. 9:10; Job 28:28) 99
20. The Last Seat In The Lifeboat (John 15:13) 103
21. The Beatles Were Wrong (Heb. 12:6) 107

22. Works-Based Parenting (Ps. 46:10)   111
23. Nothing Less Than Warfare (1 Sam. 15:23, Eph. 6:12) 115
24. No Pain, No Gain (Heb. 12:11)   119
25. False Teachings (2 Tim. 4:3)   123
26. False Teachings, Part Two (Matt. 7:15)   129
27. Love Unconditional (Rom. 3:23–24)   135
28. Monkey, Monkey, Who's Got The Monkey? (Gen. 3:16–17) 139
29. Because You Say So! (Eph. 6:1)   143
30. The Narrow Parenting Gate (Matt. 7:13–14)   147
31. Parenting Transformation (Rom. 12:2–3)   151
32. The Problem With "Christian" Parenting (James 1:22) 155
33. Nothing To Fear But Fear Itself (Phil. 4:6–7)   159
34. Focus On The Horizon (Prov. 29:18)   163
35. Idolatry Strikes Deep (Rom. 1:25; Lev. 26:1; Rev. 3:2) 167
36. Child Labor Is Still Legal! (Exod. 20:8–10)   171
37. Be The Truth And Parent On! (Prov. 15:1)   175
38. A Constant Leaning Post (Prov. 3:5–6)   179
39. A Shield And Refuge For These Times (2 Sam. 22:31) 183
40. Sin Is An Equal Opportunity Employer! (Gen. 3:6) 189

Epilogue—Lessons Learned The Hard Way   193

PREFACE

The title of this book does not refer, as one might initially think, to a parenting cryptogram your author discovered hidden in the Bible. This is not one of those dubious works. Furthermore, God would have no rational reason for concealing His design for child-rearing, and God is a super-rational Being. I use the word *code* in its usual sense, to refer to a system of principles or rules that govern a certain activity or define a certain role—both, in this case.

The members of any well-run organization—military, corporate, civic, educational—operate according to a code of conduct that sets boundaries around and defines proper individual behavior in keeping with the organization's mission. As one might expect, the Bible sets forth more than a few such codes of conduct, beginning with the commandments God gave Moses on Mount Sinai. The Bible describes codes for marriage, worship, interpersonal relationships, and yes, the Bible also describes a code for the rearing—or "training up" (the usual biblical term)—of children.

The Bible parenting code consists of hundreds of verses—far more than space herein will allow—that do not, in most cases, mention parents or children explicitly, but are nonetheless pertinent to a proper understanding of children and parental responsibilities. God is the author of the Bible's parenting code; therefore, it is impeccable. It describes the one and only proper way to raise a child. Because it is God-given, parents deviate from it at their, and their children's, peril. Unfortunately, such deviation has, since the 1960s, become the norm, even in the Christian community. Its foremost symptom is provocative misbehavior—tantrums, defiance, and disrespect of authority being the most common manifestations. In every case, we are talking about typical toddler behaviors that are present well past toddlerhood. Post-toddlerhood behavior problems have increased dramatically since the 1960s, when American parents began taking direction from so-called "experts" in the mental health professions (of which your author, ironically, is one). That body of secular parenting advice has had a disastrous effect on the behavior and mental health of children. And because it is anti-biblical in every respect, professional parenting advice has caused the relatively simple process of raising a child to be highly stressful for many if not most parents.

Since the 1960s, child discipline has become a highly controversial, even divisive, matter. The lack of general agreement on the subject has caused marriages to fail, extended family relationships to fall apart, friendships to crash and burn, and neighbors to stop speaking to one another. It has triggered conflicts between parents and teachers and caused many promising young people to leave the teaching profession. Meanwhile, mental health professionals have profited greatly from assigning bogus diagnoses to, conducting bogus therapies with, and prescribing dangerous medications for children, the ultimate victims of these disagreements.

America desperately needs a restoration of traditional, biblical child-rearing norms and practices. Such a restoration requires a road-map. Hopefully, this book will serve that purpose. Undoubtedly, the great majority of its audience will identify as Christian, but the book is not for Christians only. I am not attempting to persuade the reader to believe in the Lordship of Christ Jesus. My intent is to reach out to all who share concern for the direction child-rearing has taken since the 1960s and are willing to participate in bringing about a necessary course correction.

God's perfect parenting plan is comprised of scriptures that explicitly refer to children and parental responsibilities as well as scriptures that are not so explicit but are nonetheless relevant to those topics. This book takes a close look at forty—a good biblical number—of them (not including the Epilogue), the intention being that the reader will focus on one scripture per week over approximately nine months, but that is by no means a requirement. You can read all forty in one sitting, given sufficient mental stamina.

Each chapter is an essay. I have sequenced them in what seems to be a logical order, but you can read them in any order that suits your fancy. After reading a chapter essay:

a. ***contemplate*** how the Bible verse in question applies to you, your children, and the specifics of your family situation, especially any difficulties you may be experiencing.

b. ***communicate*** your thoughts to your spouse or "parenting partner," who is hopefully reading this book as well, and engage him or her in creative discussion.

c. ***determine*** changes you need to make in your parenting approach.

d. ***formulate*** a plan of action based on the Bible verse in question.

e. ***incorporate*** your plan into your day-to-day parenting, resolving to form new, biblical parenting behavior that gradually replaces behavior that may be the worldly norm but is not working for you.

The questions and thought exercises at the end of each chapter serve as a catalyst and guide for letting God's Word transform you into a confident, relaxed, authoritative mom or dad. It is also my hope that this book will be used to stimulate study, discussion, and discovery in church-based parent education programs (in which case, the number of chapter essays can be adjusted to fit the length of a class).

My purpose is to help you, the reader, connect with God's design for us, His most special and beloved creation, as regards the raising of His most precious children and help you experience the fullness of joy that He wants all parents to experience.

Amen!

INTRODUCTION

You are the God who works wonders; you have made known
your might among the peoples.

—Psalm 77:14 (ESV)

Ask, and it shall be given you; seek, and ye shall find; knock,
and it shall be opened unto you. For every one that asketh,
receiveth; and he that seeketh, findeth; and to him that
knocketh, it shall be opened.

—Matthew 7:7–8 (KJV)

When people think of miracles, they usually have in mind events that
have no scientific explanation; events, therefore, of supernatural nature—
Jesus walking on the stormy waters of the Sea of Galilee, for example,
or raising Lazarus from death to life. Indeed, occurrences of that sort
are miracles, but Scripture itself, being of supernatural origin, is itself a
bona fide miracle. Consider, for example, that the book of Genesis begins
with a statement of scientific fact: to wit, the universe came into being
as an inconceivably immense burst of light (Gen. 1:3), popularly known
as the Big Bang. In the first few seconds of the Big Bang, so-called dark
matter separated from light matter, an astrophysical fact described in
Genesis 1:4. (When reading this scripture, consider that God has not yet
formed the sun, moon, and stars, so the words *night* and *day* as used in

this verse do not mean daytime and nighttime.) Moses describes planet Earth as initially covered in water, a primal state that scientists have verified. As Israeli astrophysicist Gerald Schroeder (*The Science of God*, 2009) has pointed out, the creation sequence described in Genesis for days 1 through 6, culminating in God creating human beings, fits with scientific findings. The only logical explanation for how Moses—*sans* scientific instruments much less a knowledge base in astrophysics or paleontology—knew how the universe began and the precise sequence of creation is that God personally revealed it to him! That most definitely qualifies as miraculous.

One of the miracles of the Bible is that it deals with everything germane to human living. The truth of Scripture, because it is ultimate Truth, knows no boundaries—temporal, cultural, or otherwise. If one opens the Bible seeking advice on how to properly resolve a marital issue according to God's will, the Bible will become, in that person's hands, before his or her eyes, a marriage manual and a *perfect* one at that. If one comes to the Bible seeking advice on a matter of business ethics, it will become, in that person's hands, before that person's eyes, a manual on business ethics—and again, a *perfect* one. Where Judeo-Christian scripture is concerned, what one seeks, one will find, and what one finds, in every instance, is pure, unalloyed truth.

As with marital and ethical issues, if one comes to the Bible seeking advice and guidance on parenting matters, the Bible will become, in that person's hands and before his very eyes, a parenting manual. Furthermore, as with the above examples, the Bible's parenting guidance is impeccable. It is without flaw and equally applicable to every child. Human beings, however, are not without flaw. We are inclined toward sin and error in all our ways. Using God's flawless Word as one's parenting manual does not mean one will do a flawless job of raising children. It simply means one will be led in a proper direction and make considerably less error.

The following statement is an incontrovertible fact: *Imperfect human beings will do a far better job of raising children if they rely on God's perfect parenting plan than if they rely on advice and guidance provided by other imperfect human beings.*

That, in a nutshell, explains why today's parents are having so many more problems than did parents of several generations ago. In the 1960s, America unplugged from God's Word when it came to the raising of children (along with just about everything else) and plugged instead into a brand-new, untested body of parenting advice based on never-verified (and still unverified) psychological theory. As the influence of that theory-based advice has increased, so have America's child-rearing problems. Correlation does not prove cause, but correlation can be evidence of cause. In this case, correlation and cause-and-effect are one and the same. Psychological parenting theory threw American parenting off the biblical beaten path, and parents have been wandering, directionless, ever since.

Today's young parents are experiencing problems with their children that their great-grandparents—generally speaking, folks who raised children in the 1950s and before—could not have imagined. Those old-timers could not have imagined belligerent defiance on the part of preschool children ever being commonplace. They could not have imagined school-age children throwing full-blown hissy fits in the classroom and public places. They would have scoffed at the absurdity of reasonably intelligent four-year-old children acting as if they cannot fathom the purpose of a toilet. The list goes on. The current state of parenting affairs is bad for children, parents, schools, churches, communities, and culture. It is bad for everyone and everything. It bodes ill for America.

American parents need to get back on the proper parenting path, the one laid out by God in His Word. God has provided parents with a perfect parenting plan. Understanding that plan does not require a doctorate in divinity. It reveals itself to all who seek it. Furthermore, unlike the post-1960s psychological paradigm, God's plan is simple to understand and execute. Best of all, it benefits all concerned.

Why did most parents of two-plus generations ago seem so relaxed in their approach to child-rearing, and why is that no longer the case? Because the former relied, whether wittingly or not, on scripture-based principles while the greater number of today's parents—including many parents who sincerely identify as Bible-believing Christians—are relying on parenting direction based on psychological falsehoods. Thus, their parenting paths are not straight (Prov. 3:6). Thus, they are almost constantly coping with one problem or another. In turn, they experience frequent episodes of parenting stress in the form of frustration, anxiety, and guilt. Ironically, when said parents arrive at the ends of their proverbial ropes, they are inclined to seek help from psychologists—people who represent the very source of their problems.

Your author is a duly licensed psychologist; therefore, I absolutely know that the following statement is true: *Psychology is the most atheistic profession ever developed, and intentionally so.* I am by no means saying that all psychologists are atheists. I am, however, asserting that psychology is a secular philosophy that attempts to explain human behavior in terms that oppose a biblical understanding of human beings. Psychology scoffs, for example, at the idea of congenital sin. According to psychology, human beings are born pure, unsullied, without fault—moral blank slates, if you will. They do bad things, not because they come into the world bearing an innate proclivity toward doing bad things, but because their pure natures are corrupted by bad parenting and other "traumatic" life experiences (few of which were considered traumatic before psychologists defined them as such).

Furthermore, and most important, every single one of the psychologists responsible for modern psychological thought—and therefore modern parenting theory—was a radical atheist. That includes B. F. Skinner, the psychologist behind the behavior modification theory that informs today's failed approach to child discipline. It includes Abraham Maslow and Carl Rogers, the humanistic psychologists responsible for the demonic lie that high regard (esteem) for oneself is the brass ring of *la dolce vita*. It includes Sigmund Freud, the so-called "Father of Modern Psychology," who is on record as saying that people who believe in a Supreme Supernatural Being are mentally ill. There are no exceptions to the psychology-is-an-atheistic-philosophy rule. Psychology is based on cleverly phrased falsehoods. As such, it qualifies as an example of the "deceptive philosophies" Paul warned of in his epistle to the Colossians (2:8; see this book's chapter 3).

It should go without saying that human beings cannot be properly understood by someone who eliminates our Creator from the equation.

As such, a psychologist's ability to be helpful is seriously compromised (and that applies as well to a significant number of so-called Christian psychologists). Researchers have found, for example, that most people who seek psychological counseling do not obtain better emotional and mental health. On average, of three people who see psychologists because of troubles in their lives, one becomes even more troubled and one testifies to no change, leaving but one who claims benefit. Would you see a medical doctor with a similar record? How about an auto mechanic?

Take it from one who is a member (albeit heretical) of the club, psychology is a secular religion that one believes in by faith. It has a priesthood, doctrine, supposedly "healing" rituals, idols, and inquisitions. But the characteristic that most qualifies psychology as a religion is its promise that a human being can be regenerated—cleansed of negative, self-destructive thoughts, habits, and emotions—through a process conducted by another person who also suffers, as do all human beings, from negative and self-destructive thoughts, habits, and emotions. The proposition is absurd on its face. Authentic transformation occurs through Christ and Christ alone.

Regarding the raising of children, psychology has been a wrecking ball. Since American parents began taking their marching orders from mental health professionals, the *per capita* expansion of the profession of child and adolescent psychology has outpaced every other health-care field. Meanwhile, every indicator of positive mental health in America's children has gone (and is still going) steadily downhill. School achievement is considerably lower. The lives of many teens are perpetual personal soap operas marked by one "issue" and "trigger event" after another. The child and teen suicide rate is ten times what it was in the early 1960s. A significant number of today's kids are even anxious and confused concerning the gender to which God assigned them.

A journalist once asked me if there was *anything* about post-1960s psychological parenting that improved over pre-1960s traditional child-rearing.

My answer: "No, nothing. Wrong thinking leads to dysfunctional, counterproductive behavior. Psychological parenting has been a disaster for everyone except psychologists, who have profited greatly from the destruction their bogus theories, diagnoses, and therapies have wrought."

The person asking the question was thinking that perhaps we could take some aspects of old-fashioned, Bible-based child-rearing and some aspects of modern psychological parenting, put them together, and come up a hybrid superior to both. But there is absolutely nothing redeemable about psychological parenting theory. We need to dispose of it, all of it. There is no third path between traditional, biblical child-rearing and the pseudo-scientific parenting paradigm that has gripped America since the 1960s.

God's child-rearing plan (and, therefore, His plan for the family) is simple. It is free of theory and confirmed by common sense. Interesting enough, and paradoxically, God's child-rearing plan is also corroborated by social science research. Literally, it makes *perfect* sense. And because the architect of said parenting design is the Great Architect Himself, it works! And that, when all is said and done, is what truly matters.

1
HISTORY REPEATS ITSELF

But the LORD came down to see the city and the tower the
people were building. The LORD said, "If as one people speaking
the same language they have begun to do this, then nothing
they plan to do will be impossible for them. Come, let us go
down and confuse their language so they will not understand
each other."

—*Genesis 11:5–7*

Since its inception, the purveyors of postmodern psychological parenting have produced more than one hundred thousand books promoting
their progressive theories. To put that into perspective, if said books
are one-inch thick on average and were carefully placed one atop
another, the resulting stack of books would reach 8,333 feet into the
clouds! As of 2021, the world's tallest building—the Burj Khalifa
in Dubai—is 2,717 feet tall. Fancy that! Our hypothetical stack of
parenting books is slightly more than three times the height of the
world's tallest building!

I call that imaginary stack of books the Tower of Parent-Babble.
The reference, of course, is to the story of the Tower of Babel (Gen.
11). That peculiar tale begins with all of mankind speaking one language and being of one purpose, however mischievous it was. When

God sees the massive structure they are building, intending to reach the heavens and "make a name for [themselves]," He confuses their language such that they are no longer able to understand one another and, therefore, accomplish a common purpose. With that, God puts a stop to their grandiose project and scatters them across the face of the earth.

I am a member of the last generation of children to be raised by adults who were of one mind when it came to children. In the 1950s, the decade of my childhood, it was rare to find a husband and wife who did not agree concerning their kids. In addition, parents agreed with their children's teachers. A child who got into trouble at school got into even more trouble at home. His or her explanation of what had happened never trumped the teacher's report. When it came to children, neighbors agreed. Parents of different faiths agreed. Even parents of no faith agreed with parents of faith!

It was not so long ago that nearly everyone in America was on the same child-rearing page—one defined by biblical principles. Back then, the primary aim of rearing a child was that of producing a good citizen, which everyone agreed was accomplished by teaching right from wrong—instilling, in other words, a functional moral compass. In that regard, even atheists agreed that right and wrong were defined by universal principles set forth in the Ten Commandments (or at least Commandments 5 through 10, those referring to one's obligations to parents and neighbors). In effect, everyone spoke the same child-rearing "language."

Then, as the 1960s waned, members of the mental health professions—psychologists mostly—began claiming, in one voice, that traditional child-rearing was harmful to a child's psyche. Supposedly, that time-honored approach caused children to repress traumatic memories, hide their true feelings, and not be capable of independent thought. Mind you, the mental health community advanced these ludicrous assertions without a shred of confirming evidence. (Take my word for it, folks, we are talking about some of the most intellectually arrogant people in the human-sphere.) Nonetheless, because the public (a) tends to be somewhat awed by psychologists and (b) believes that capital letters after one's name means the person in question is an expert, mental health professionals were able to persuade parents to abandon tried-and-true child-rearing and embrace an untested philosophy founded on one falsehood after another.

The new experts also promoted the idea that a child's upbringing needed to be defined by his or her "individual differences." Eventually, most of these supposed differences were transformed into diagnoses, the most notorious of which are attention-deficit/hyperactivity disorder (ADHD), oppositional defiant disorder (ODD), and early-onset bipolar disorder (EOBD, albeit its nomenclature changes every few years). In short order, one child-rearing language became many. As various forms of parent-speak proliferated, child-rearing confusion set in and parents were no longer able to understand and relate to one another.

"Well," one parent says to another, "you just don't understand what it's like to live with a child who is ADHD. His therapist says that normal means of discipline aren't going to work with him."

"Our adoption specialist has told us that we must parent Suzie with the trauma of her adoption uppermost in mind," says the mother of a hyper-petulant eight-year-old who was adopted at birth. (Adoption only became "traumatic" for adoptees when psychologists said it was.)

Yet another parent claims that her five-year-old "has a sensory disorder that causes her to reject certain foods and requires that I cook her special meals."

In no time at all, the confusion and miscommunication of Babel was upon us once again, only this time it concerned children. In the 1950s, it was rare to find a husband and wife who could not come to agreement concerning their children. Today, many parents are not on the same page with one another, teachers, neighbors, or their children's grandparents. A significant number of said parents aren't even in the same book with one another! Today, child-rearing is called "parenting," and has been since 1970. One might think the terms are interchangeable, but they are not. As the following chart describes, the differences are profound:

Pre-1960s CHILD-REARING	Post-1960s PARENTING
Child-rearing "experts" are elders in one's extended family, church, or community	Parenting "experts" are mental health professionals
The family is adult-centered	The family is child-centered
Focus on instilling functional moral compass, a proper understanding of right *versus* wrong	Focus on assisting children toward academic, athletic, and artistic achievement
Parents teach respect for others	Parents attempt to instill high self-esteem
Parents function as authority figures	Parents attempt to be liked by their children
Children have chores	Children have activities but few chores
Children are not big deals	Children are idols
Relatively stress-free	Highly stressful, especially for women
Parents are married first, parents second	Parenting comes first, being married second
Child's behavior of paramount importance	Child's feelings of paramount importance

Two entirely different ways of regarding and approaching children will lead to two entirely different outcomes and, sure enough, the outcomes of pre-1960s child-rearing and post-1960s parenting are as different as night and day. Child-rearing is simple and straightforward. Parenting is confusing and difficult. Parenting wears people out, especially mothers. Parenting damages marriages. Parenting has decimated the mental health of children. Parenting requires expert assistance (irony noted). Parenting leads to diagnoses and prescriptions for psychiatric drugs. Post-1960s parenting is bad mojo.

This book is a clarion call for the restoration of the simple straightforwardness of mere child-rearing (albeit I reluctantly use the word *parenting* when the alternative is awkward). The restoration of mere child-rearing requires an understanding of its biblical underpinnings. I pray that this book will lead you, the reader, toward that understanding. May everyone in your family profit greatly from the retro-journey you have chosen to undertake!

FOR PERSONAL PONDERING
AND GROUP DISCUSSION

1. If to this point in your journey as a parent, you have been parenting rather than merely raising children, what difficulties have you encountered as a result? What difference(s) do you think mere child-rearing would have made?

2. If you want to stop parenting and begin raising your kids according to traditional understandings and biblical principles, what, exactly, do you need to begin doing to make the necessary course correction? (Refer to the above chart.)

3. Is there something about parenting that you feel you want to keep, and if so, why?

2

IN THE BEGINNING

Therefore shall a man leave his father and his mother and shall cleave unto his wife: and they shall be one flesh.

—*Genesis 2:24 (KJV)*

On the sixth day of creation—after creating the heavens and the earth and populating the latter with a multitude of flora and fauna—God creates Adam, the first human being. What follows is somewhat anomalous: *"And the Lord God said, 'It is not good that man should be alone'" (Gen. 2:18).*

Up to that point in the story, everything in creation has been declared by God to be "good." But He now declares that until Adam has a suitable mate, creation is yet unfinished. And so, God fashions a "helper" or "help meet" (KJV) for Adam.

Before creating Eve, however, God brings the animals to Adam to see what names he will give them. Naming the animals is Adam's first taste of having dominion over the earth (Gen. 1:26). When the parade of animals is over, it is obvious that each of them has another of its kind, "but for Adam there was not found a helper fit for him" (Gen. 2:20). God is sending Adam a message: to wit, he is not an animal. Adam is a unique creation—a *human* being. As such, his helper will not be an animal either—she cannot be, in fact. She, too, will be human, of Adam's "kind."

God then causes Adam to fall into a deep sleep, takes one of his ribs, and creates a woman (Gen. 2:22). In contemporary terms, this is a "one-off." God did not use part of a male cow to craft a female cow, part of a male hummingbird to create a female hummingbird, and so on. God's creation of a woman, a female partner for Adam, is exceptional, one of a kind (as any self-respecting woman will agree it should have been!). When he awakes, Adam immediately recognizes that he and the woman are meant for one another, that she is "bone of [his] bone and flesh of [his] flesh" (Gen. 2:23). They are intimately connected to one another and their relationship is unique in God's creation.

Verse 24 begins with "therefore"—that is, because God wrought Eve out of Adam—and goes on to describe the three-step process by which a man and a woman will leave the nuclear families in which they were raised and join in marriage. (The three *shalls* of the King James Version identify the verse as an imperative.)

- First, a man *shall* emancipate himself ("leave his father and mother")
- Second, the man *shall* emancipate and marry a woman ("cleave unto his wife")
- Third, the man and woman *shall* "be one flesh."

Mind you, the phrase "one flesh" refers not just to a relationship in which husband and wife are sexually faithful, but one of philosophical, spiritual, and emotional union. According to God's design, husband and wife are to be of one worldview, one purpose, one accord. In God's design, the marital bond is much more than simply "skin deep." The term "one flesh" means the husband–wife relationship is both sanctified and exclusive. Theirs is the one and only relationship in which a state of *one flesh* is possible. To be blunt, two men or two women who are "married" according to a man-contrived law are not and cannot ever enter a biblical state of one flesh. God did not create another man from Adam's rib. He created woman from man, and that, folks, is that—the end of the story, so to speak.

Being of one flesh means husband and wife are sexually monogamous, of one accord, and possessing of one worldview, but it also means—and this is equally important—that *neither of them allow any other purpose (e.g., a job) or relationship, even one that is non-sexual, to eclipse or displace their husband–wife relationship.*

Unfortunately, in the post-1960s family, the husband–wife relationship is often found playing second fiddle to the relationship between parent(s) and child or children. An interesting exercise serves to illustrate the point: When I'm working with a small group of husbands and wives, I ask everyone to fill in the two blanks in the following sentence:

> ***In the last week or so, of the time I spent with my family, I spent ___ percent of time in the role of either husband or wife and ___ percent of time in the role of either father or mother.***

On average, parents who take this exercise answer that they spend 10 percent of their family time in the role of spouse and 90 percent of that time in the role of parent. Some even admit that they generally spend *zero* percent of their time occupying the role of husband or wife! I have conducted this exercise hundreds of times. Every time, the average percentages have been approximately the same. In other words, whether raised by Christian or secular parents, the typical child:

- is not seeing what a proper, godly marriage *looks like.*
- is not being taught the significance of the husband–wife relationship.
- is being taught, implicitly, that he or she is the most important person in the family—effectively, an idol.

That is not good in the least. It means that in the typical American family, the male and female adults are:

- talking more to their kids than with one another.
- paying more attention to their kids than to one another.
- more interested in their kids than in one other.
- more thoughtful, considerate, helpful, positive, affirming, polite, and encouraging toward their kids than they are toward one another.

At this point, the three most important questions the reader can ask him- or herself are (a) "Does the above list of characteristics describe me/us to significant degree?"; (b) "Have my spouse and I, however unintentionally, created a child-centered family?"; and (c) "Are my spouse and I sending the wrong messages to our kids?" If your answers are *yes, yes, and yes,* you are by no means alone. Unfortunately, the upside-down, inside-out, turned around backwards family has become the norm since the 1960s. A fact to consider:

> *Nothing puts a more solid foundation of well-being under a child than the knowledge that his parents are in a committed union, a relationship that obviously transcends in both quality and quantity either of their relationships with him. (The application of this principle to single parenting can be found below.)*

All too often in today's parenting culture, a man and a woman marry, have children, and begin acting as if they exchanged the following vow on their wedding day: "I take you to be my husband/wife until *children* do us part." The more they "parent," the more their marriage slips into the background and the more likely it becomes that child-idolatry will become the substitute. The husband and wife in question are not in a state of unity with one another as much as they are with their kids. Their intentions are good, mind you. After all, they are only trying to be the best parents they can possibly be (according to worldly standards). The problem is that a person's intentions do not necessarily determine the outcome of something he does. The most pertinent question becomes: "Are a person's intentions and behavior in line with God's life-design for human beings, or are they not?"

If intentions, behavior, and God's life-design line up, fine. But in this case, the intention to be the best parent one can possibly be and the resulting over-focus on one's children do not begin to line up with God's life-design for human beings.

It cannot be emphasized enough: In God's design for the human family, the roles of father and mother are intended to be *secondary* to the roles of husband and wife. No parenting variable—even a child with life-threatening special needs—justifies putting the roles of father and mother in front of the roles of husband and wife.

The reader may be asking, "Concerning the illuminating exercise above, what, ideally, should the percentages be?"

Good question. There is no sound reason why they should deviate significantly from 85 percent husband/wife and 15 percent father/mother. (Note: The unique, labor-intensive nature of a child's first two years of life allow for adjusting those figures to around 60/40.) Ironically, children should be raised *not* by fathers and mothers but by people who are occupying, to the greatest extent possible, the God-sanctioned roles of husband and wife.

CAVEAT

It should be obvious that the 85/15 rule does not apply to single parents. Nonetheless, it is imperative that single parents limit the time they spend being child-oriented. Single parents need relationships, recreations, and responsibilities that offset the potential perils (to both parent and children) of over-focusing on the kids.

God wants children to be a delight. And in that regard, the Bible does indeed refer to the roles of father and mother, but when a child emancipates (as instructed in Gen. 2:24), God intends for the marriage that produced the child to still be vibrant. In a family where the marriage has always been *número uno,* the roles of husband and wife do not have to be recovered (regenerated, resuscitated, restored) after children leave home. One does not need to find what has not been misplaced.

The following fact is also pertinent to this discussion:

A person who departs from God's design in how he lives his life is going to bring down trouble on his head.

When parenting takes priority over marriage, the trouble comes in the form of children who are insecure, which they express through disobedience, disrespect, moodiness, petulance, and chronic irresponsibility. Insecure children often develop mental health issues like drug and alcohol use, depression, anxiety, cutting, and addiction to social media or video games. For parents, the trouble comes in the form of stress, anxiety, self-doubt, guilt, anger, resentment, fear, and other forms of mental anguish caused by parenting difficulties. Almost without exception, the trouble comes in the form of arguments between parents concerning parenting issues. In that regard, I am frequently asked, "How can my spouse and I get on the same page concerning the kids?"

The reason—in my experience, the one and only reason—that a husband and wife are not on the same page concerning their children is they are failing to act primarily as husband and wife; instead, they are acting primarily as father and mother. Remember, being of one flesh means more than simply being sexually faithful. It also means being of one point of view. In effect, Genesis 2:24 says, ironically, that it is virtually impossible for a husband and a wife to occupy the same parenting page if their default roles are father and mother. In that event, the problem of not being on the same parenting page is not going to be solved by any of the stock solutions proposed by marriage and family therapists: listening better to one another, having greater appreciation for one another's feelings, learning to compromise with one another, going out on a date every Friday night. Those "solutions" are way off base. They fail to recognize the root of the problem.

My answer to a person who asks how to get on the same page with his or her spouse: "You need to get married."

"But John," the person will invariably say (taking the bait), "we are married!"

"No, you're really not," I then say. "Being married means much more than simply having a certificate issued by a clerk of court. Marriage is a spiritual condition. People who are truly, spiritually married never, ever ask the question you just asked. You have allowed the roles of father and mother to take over your home. Instead of father and mother being part-time jobs, they've swallowed up your entire lives."

God's design for the family requires that husband and wife be the dominant adult roles in a family. The problem, of course, is that being dad and mom first is the way of the world. As such, people who conduct themselves in their families according to God's design are in danger of being thought of by their peers as "weird." But then, I cannot think of a better way to live than being "weird for Christ."

FOR PERSONAL PONDERING AND GROUP DISCUSSION

1. Is your home child-centric versus adult-centric? If your family orbits around your kids, can you identify how that happened and how it has affected your marriage, your children's behavior, and your own well-being?
2. Are you willing to be weird, meaning out of step with the world? What are some concrete ways you can restore your marriage as the centerpiece of your family, its rightful status?
3. How do the principles and advice contained in this chapter apply to single parenthood? What is the equivalent, for example, of marriage-centeredness in a single-parent home?

3
FOOL'S GOLD

See to it that no one takes you captive by philosophy and empty deceit, according to human tradition, according to the elemental spirits of the world, and not according to Christ.

—Colossians 2:8

In the 1950s, when I was being raised by a single mom and then her and her second husband, the number of parenting books in the marketplace could have been counted on one hand. Furthermore, those few manuals were not actually "parenting" books in the post-1960s sense of the term. They dealt primarily with practical matters like breastfeeding *versus* bottle-feeding and how to recognize and deal with colic and various childhood maladies of the day, like chicken pox. The authors in question assumed an audience consisting of responsible adults who understood that children needed firm authority in their lives. When it came to specific discipline problems, those same folks understood that if common sense did not quite pan out, then advice from one's elders probably would. Taking the most prominent example, pediatrician Benjamin Spock devoted less than 5 percent of his mega-seller, *The Common Sense Book of Baby and Child Care* (1946), to advice on handling misbehavior.

As I write, it has been seventy-five years since Spock's book was first published. Since then, more than one hundred thousand parenting books have infiltrated the marketplace. Many of those works have been written by people who, like yours truly, are mental health professionals of one sort or another: psychologists, clinical social workers, family therapists, behavioral specialists, and so on. A sizeable percentage of these works deal primarily with the issue of discipline. Unfortunately, one can no longer assume that even the most responsible parents are clear on a child's need for firm authority. Nor can it be assumed that loving parents are in possession of common sense when it comes to their children or that they will give even two cents for child-rearing advice from their elders. The problem does not originate with parents, however, but with America's ultra-progressive mental health community.

American parents began taking their marching orders from mental health professionals in the late 1960s. As psychobabble replaced common sense, every statistic on child mental health went into a nosedive that has been ongoing since (as, mind you, the per-child number of mental health professionals has increased more than one-thousand-fold). The only sensible conclusion: *When it comes to children, mental health professional advice has been a disaster.* As a group, mental health professionals may be slightly smarter than the average bear, but they look at children and child-rearing through a "glass, darkly" (1 Cor. 13:12)— through the distorting, obfuscating filter of (unverified) psychological theory. Noteworthy is the fact that the theory in question—without exception—was formulated by people who denied the reality of God. The inevitable result of denying God and the truth of His Word is a body of advice that creates more problems than it solves, as exemplified by the ever-escalating post-1960s child and teen mental health crisis.

Examples of the difference between child-rearing advice based on biblical principle versus that based on psychological theory:

- God's Word warns against self-esteem (Matt. 23:12, chapter 18); mental health professionals claim that self-esteem is essential to a child's mental health.
- God instructs parents to discipline their children as powerfully as they love them (Prov. 3:12); mental health professionals downplay and even demonize discipline, especially in punitive forms.

- God says that discipline is not effective if it does not cause a child emotional discomfort (Heb. 12:11); mental health professionals eschew any form of discipline that causes a child guilt, shame, or remorse and, therefore, prompts genuine atonement.
- God says children are sinful by nature (Ps. 51:5); mental health professionals maintain that a child's fundamental goodness would be never-ending if it were not for wrong-headed parenting and other bad influences and experiences in his life.

By biblical standards, psychology is a deceit, a fraud. It consists of propositions concerning the nature and needs of human beings, all of which—no exceptions here, either—stand in one-hundred-eighty-degree opposition to a biblical understanding of human nature and needs. For that simple reason, psychology qualifies as one of the deceitful philosophies Paul prophetically warned of in his letter to the Christians in Colossae. Unfortunately—tragically, even—American parents were taken captive by the deceits of psychological parenting theory in the late 1960s and have been captives since. Furthermore, the deceit has been so thoroughly effective that many parents, if confronted with it, do not recognize themselves as its captives.

One of Satan's primary targets is the family. Since the 1960s, he has used psychological parenting theory to sow discord (between husband and wife), disrespect (of child for parents), and disobedience (of child toward parents, teachers, and other adult authorities) into the family, school, and community. There is but one solution to this seductive and destructive guile: the restoration, one family at a time, of a godly parenting point of view and godly parenting practices. Are you ready to join the retro-revolution?

FOR PERSONAL PONDERING AND GROUP DISCUSSION

1. In raising your children, can you identify at least one deceitful psychological theory that has caused you unnecessary difficulty? Do you, for example, praise your children lavishly, thinking that "positive reinforcement" is essential to their possessing high self-esteem? If so, how has that played out?

2. How would your parenting look today if you had not fallen for psychological theory and had, instead, completely embraced God's instructions and principles when it came to raising your kids?

3. What can you begin doing differently, today, to bring your child-rearing practices into better alignment with God's design? Will you? Are you willing to swim against the tide?

4
FOUNDATIONS

When even the foundations are being destroyed, what can the righteous do?

—Psalm 11:3

A worldview is a philosophy of life; a mental framework with which a person organizes and understands his life and life in general, mankind, and the universe. An individual's worldview consists, therefore, of answers to the following questions:

- Why do I exist?
- What is life's purpose?
- How did the universe come into existence?
- What are my gifts and how should I use them?
- What are my limitations and how should I deal with them?
- What are my responsibilities to others?
- Does God exist, and if so, how does that affect my answers to the preceding questions?

A person's worldview is comprised of his or her fundamental beliefs. A Christian worldview begins with belief in the one God who—as described in the opening chapters of the Bible's first book, Genesis—created the universe, the earth, and all forms of life, including human beings. A Christian worldview proceeds from those Old Testament roots to encompass belief in Christ Jesus and the saving work He accomplished on the Cross for anyone who comes to profess Him.

Every worldview, even those which are in error, is grounded in certain essential understandings, assumptions, creeds, and practices that distinguish it from others. These essentials are a worldview's defining cornerstones. The foundation of a Christian worldview rests on four such cornerstones:

1. Love of God and His Son, Christ Jesus
2. Love of neighbor
3. Love between husband and wife
4. Love of children

The first of the four is, of course, the primary or—as the Bible puts it—*chief* cornerstone (Acts 4:10–12). Both the first and second cornerstones correspond to what Jesus identified as the first and second great commandments (Matt. 22:37–39, chapters 9 and 10). The third cornerstone was laid in the garden, when God created Eve to be Adam's wife and commanded them to be true to one another (Gen. 2:24, chapter 2).

The fourth cornerstone represents the primary purpose of marriage: child-rearing. In God's plan, husband and wife are to raise children in accord with His "training and instruction" (Eph. 6:4, chapter 15). Biblical child-rearing ensures, to the greatest degree possible, that children, when they become adults, will love God and His Son, love their neighbors, create strong marriages, and raise children according to God's plan. In this fashion, every Christian generation renews, re-strengthens, and reenergizes Christian culture, thus laying the foundation for the coming of His kingdom.

Satan's overarching purpose is to weaken and ultimately replace those self-transcending loves with love of self. Humanists—atheists who place ever-evolving materialistic man at the center of their debased worldview—employ the synonyms self-realization, self-actualization, self-sufficiency, and self-esteem. Since the 1960s, humanism's influence has been increasing in American culture, evidence of which includes the Supreme Court's ban on school prayer in 1962, the wholesale legalization of abortion on demand in 1973, the normalization of homosexuality beginning in the late 1960s, the transformation of public schools into indoctrination centers for humanist values, and most recently, the irrational notion that a person's gender is "fluid" and subject to personal whim. In every case, man's sinful way has trumped (for the moment, at least) God's way. In fact, humanists believe that since God is a fiction, any conversation about His "way," "plan," or "design" is patently absurd. To the card-carrying humanist, there is man's way and there is nature's way, and a state of universal spiritual perfection will be achieved when the former finally conforms itself to the latter. That, in a nutshell, defines humanist eschatology—the utopian notion that human beings are evolving toward a state of spiritual "oneness" with unspoiled nature. A lovely thought, but then Satan is a very clever fellow.

To a humanist, the young child epitomizes that ideal. The young child is, in effect, a role model whose (supposed) attributes—moral innocence, non-judgmentalism, and natural desire to live in harmony with nature—should become ideals for adults. Humanists are in blissful denial of the facts: to wit, the young child is through no fault of his or her own a self-centered, emotionally driven, pre-sociopath who believes that what he wants, he deserves to have and because he *deserves* what he wants, the ends justify the means. The toddler is the epitome of self-love; nonetheless, humanists believe anyone who does not see children through their rose-colored glasses is mean-spirited. Because it idealizes and idolizes children, humanism downplays the need to discipline them. Point of fact: the reality that children require firm discipline is 100 percent incompatible with the most foundational of humanist notions— that man's congenital makeup includes a drive toward moral goodness. Given the constraints of their worldview and "human-view," humanists have no choice but to reject the notion that children require "the rod of discipline" to expunge inborn "foolishness" from their hearts (Prov. 22:15, chapter 13).

An example of humanist thought concerning children and child-rearing was featured in a December 2019 online article by Hunter Clarke-Fields (HCF), a self-described "mindfulness parenting coach." Clarke-Fields argued against punishing children when they misbehave, citing "many" other researchers—conveniently unnamed except for Alan Kazdin, director of the Yale Parenting Center. According to Clarke-Fields, Kazdin, et al., have discovered that punishment causes all manner of mental and emotional harm to children. To believe HCF is to believe that punishment completely ruins a child's life, turning him into a self-loathing, emotionally stunted wreck. Let me assure the reader that the research referred to by HCF does not qualify as research at all, not unless cutting ludicrous ideas out of whole cloth so qualifies. Humanism, because its chief cornerstone has "GOD IS A RIDICULOUS BUT EVIL FICTION!" carved deeply into it, consists of nothing but fictions. Humanists dress their fabrications in words like "research" because the truth would expose them for the charlatans that they are—the truth being that they compulsively make things up. They are propagandists, not scientists.

In her online article, HCF is cleverly building a case for dumbing down the legal definition of child abuse to include punishment—any punishment—for misbehavior. After all, if society is to ever be perfected, the necessary social engineering must begin with government-appointed "experts" dictating how children are "parented." Despite their claims to the effect that humanism is a philosophy of concern and respect for all mankind, humanists are dangerous people with a dangerous agenda that will be, if ever implemented, extremely destructive.

In October 2019, pastor and theologian John Piper wrote and posted to his website at DesiringGod.org an article titled "Parents, Require Obedience of Your Children." Piper makes the point that by abdicating their rightful, God-assigned authority over their children and failing to teach their kids the joy of submission to legitimate authority, parents are condemning their children to eternal death, handing them over to Satan. His article is a plea to Christian parents that they step up to the proverbial plate concerning the urgent need to teach their kids to walk in the way of God's Word, in submission to His Son. Piper is pleading because, like most people our age (he and I were born about two years apart), he has seen, with the clarity that comes from having been raised by people who properly understood their responsibilities to God and neighbor, the steady advance of the enemy. Piper is worried and feels compelled to sound an alarm.

Piper says he understands why parents who embrace secular humanism do not discipline their children but is unable to understand why that has become true of many Christian parents as well. I think he does understand. Piper—known for his cultural critiques as well as his apologetics—knows as well as I that no small number of people who identify as Christians and even attend church regularly are not steadfast when it comes to their faith. Many are those who say they are Christian and yet wobble down the wide path of the world. Folks who profess Christ but do not follow Him down the hardest and narrowest of all roads are found sitting in church every Sunday morning.

The question remains: When the foundations are being destroyed, what are the righteous supposed to do? The righteous are to do what is right. To employ a popular exhortation from the late 1960s, we are to keep on truckin'. We are to press on. We are to head straight into the storm with our heads held high. We are to never give up; never surrender. We are to love God, His Son, our neighbors (even the most annoying and provocative of them), our parents (in spite of their warts), our spouses, and our children (even the most irritating and rebellious of them). We are to be custodians of the cornerstones, defenders of the foundations. We are to safeguard, preserve, maintain, uphold.

I happen to be a member of the last generation of American children to be raised (for the most part) according to biblical principle. We are known as Baby Boomers. In most cases, we were born after World War II, attended school in the 1950s and early 1960s, and emancipated in our late teens and early twenties. Even those of us whose parents were not believers will agree that our parents subscribed, however unwittingly, to biblical principle. When we went to school, we encountered teachers who subscribed likewise. As I tell folks, I did not attend a Christian school, but I attended a school that overtly promoted Christian values.

Most of us Boomers came to first grade not knowing as much as our ABCs. Our mothers did not sit with us while we did our homework, making sure we did everything without error. They expected us, from an early age, to accept full responsibility for the things that "belonged" to us, one of which was our school performance. When we did something wrong in the neighborhood or in school, our parents did not come to our defense, claiming extenuating circumstances or denying that we were even capable of misdeed. Far from it. They volunteered for the firing squad.

In the home, our parents' authority was not questioned. They said, "Do this," and we did it. They said, "You better not do this," and we did whatever it was at our peril. Our parents' stock answer to "Why?" or "Why not?" was "Because I said so." Our moms and dads stood together when it came to us. They were on the same page, in the same paragraph even, simply because they occupied the roles of husband and wife to a much greater extent than they occupied the roles of mom and dad.

The outcome of this virtually bygone state of affairs:

- By the end of first grade—even first grades consisting of fifty students and one teacher (as was mine)—we boomers were reading at a higher level than post-1960s first-grade graduates, and we outperformed them at every grade level.
- Our mental health, as measured by the child and teen suicide rate per capita, was at least ten times better than the mental health of today's kids.
- We emancipated much earlier and much more successfully than today's young adults.
- We did not need so-called "safe spaces" when we went to college.

Since the 1960s, there has been a steady drift away from biblical principles in America's homes and schools. As that drift has occurred, childhood behavior problems have gone markedly up, and child mental health has gone markedly down. These troubling trends are happening because American parenting lacks a sturdy anchor. Along with many other things about America, we lost our child-rearing moorings in the late 1960s and early 1970s and have been adrift ever since.

If America's child-rearing problems are going to be corrected, they are going to be corrected in homes where God's Word sits center stage. The Christian home is ground zero for this battle, and believe me, it is going to be a battle. Satan is not going to sit idly by as parents reclaim the right course. When it comes to America's ubiquitous child-rearing problems, the secular home is a goner. The secular home has no road-map, no reliable guide with which to find its way back to the main road, Highway One and Only. The Christian home has that roadmap. It may have accumulated some dust, but it's still there, waiting.

Whether writing or speaking, my purpose is to help parents understand that there is but *one right way* to raise God's children: *His way*! He has laid out those instructions in His Word. His Word sits in the bookrack of nearly every church pew in America. His Word is found in nearly every Christian home in America. His Word is freely available in nearly every bookstore in America, including nearly every online bookstore.

Parents have, therefore, no excuses.

FOR PERSONAL PONDERING AND GROUP DISCUSSION

1. What would your day-to-day parenting look like if you were to stop raising your children in keeping with bogus psychological theory and the expectations of the world and set yourself to making sure God's Word is lived out in your home?
2. What would be the consequences to you personally of dedicating yourself to making sure God's Word was lived out faithfully in your family?
3. What specific, intentional things can you do in your home to maintain the Four Essential Cornerstones of a biblical worldview in a state of reasonably good repair and prepare for the coming of God's kingdom on earth?

5
WORLDVIEW

If with Christ you died to the elemental spirits of the world,
why, as if you were still alive in the world, do you submit to
regulations ... (referring to things that all perish as they are
used)—according to human precepts and teachings? These
have indeed an appearance of wisdom in promoting self-made
religion ... but they are of no value in stopping the indulgence
of the flesh.

—Colossians 2:20–23

The word *worldview* is bandied about a lot these days, but most
folks—even many who identify as social conservatives or evangelical Christians—have some difficulty defining it. They will say, for
example, that *worldview* means "the way one looks at the world" or
something similarly redundant. Let's take a moment, then, to define
it properly.

Simply, one's worldview is one's philosophy of life. Even if someone
has difficulty defining it, he possesses a philosophy, a set of beliefs and
values, that governs his actions in the world. One's philosophy of life
begins with some understanding of how the universe and, specifically,
biological life originated. A biblical worldview, therefore, begins with
the (scientifically supported) belief that the universe and all forms of

life originated with God and that God's creation process is accurately (albeit in simple terms) described in the first two chapters of Genesis. A secular worldview, by contrast, is termed *mechanistic* because it attributes the universe and biological life to impersonal, random, mechanical processes, chief among which is the (scientifically unsupported) notion that the first living cell arose spontaneously *vis a' vis* some combination of chemicals and heat during earth's infancy and began evolving from there into increasingly sophisticated life forms, eventually culminating in human beings. That atheist theory, which lacks even the smallest crumb of confirming evidence, is known as Darwinism, after its nineteenth-century formulator, Charles Darwin.

It is almost a given that someone who believes God created the universe and everything in it as described in the first chapter of Genesis also believes:

- Human beings are the crown of God's creation.
- Earth is the only planet in the universe that supports an ecosystem.
- Human beings fell from grace almost immediately by choosing to accept the serpent's deceptive sales pitch instead of obeying God's prohibition concerning the tree of knowledge of good and evil.
- God gave human beings a book, the Bible, containing both His story and mankind's story—including the story of our future, earthly and supernatural—as well as His design for living proper moral lives.
- The Ten Commandments (Exod. 20:1–17; Deut. 5:4–21) contain God's fundamental principles for worshipping Him and loving one's neighbor.
- Authentic truth is absolute and timeless; it is not a function of culture or historical time, much less individual preference. (The notion that truth is not and has never been absolute is called *moral relativism*. That is what the serpent promised Eve: that she could liberate herself from God's moral definitions and be self-sufficient.)

- The essential Christian creed is found in Jesus's words as recorded in Matthew 22:38–39: "Love God with all your heart, soul, and mind ... [and] love your neighbor as yourself."
- Jesus is the Messiah promised by the Old Testament prophets.
- Jesus is the one and only Son of God, the Son of the Trinity, sent by God the Father to offer Himself as the perfect atonement for our sin condition.
- The culmination of God's redemptive plan for mankind is described in the spiritual language of the Bible's last book, Revelation.
- Things on earth, in this life, are going to go from bad to worse, but for believers in the lordship of Christ Jesus, everything will turn out fine because heaven awaits us.

Instilling a biblical worldview into a child begins with teaching those fundamentals, along with teaching the child an understanding of how those fundamentals translate into Christian social values and behavior. The most important aspect of teaching a biblical worldview should be obvious: teaching the meaning and day-to-day application of God's Word. Other important components of instilling a biblical worldview include:

- regular church attendance;
- after church family discussion of the meaning and application of the sermon and Sunday School lessons;
- daily reading and family discussion from the Bible and devotionals;
- using the Bible as a guide when discussing life situations of whatever nature, always emphasizing that the Bible is a comprehensive and reliable guide for proper living (there being no such thing as "the Bible doesn't really address that"); and
- conducting your social life with like-minded people and encouraging your child to socialize with like-minded kids.

Preventing, to the greatest degree possible, your children from becoming swallowed up in worldly concerns like peer group popularity may well be a parent's greatest accomplishment—better even than "My child won a full academic scholarship to Harvard!"

FOR PERSONAL PONDERING AND
GROUP DISCUSSION

1. Identify where you may have fallen short in teaching a biblical worldview to your children. How have those shortfalls translated into behavior that begs for correction?
2. Where you have identified areas that need improvement, develop a plan for remediating each of those deficiencies.
3. Identify two other Bible verses that address the importance of teaching children a biblical worldview.

6
PARENTS AS GOD'S "IMAGERS"

Then God said, "Let Us make man in Our image, after Our likeness, to rule over the fish of the sea and the birds of the air and the livestock, and over all the earth itself and every creature that crawls upon it." So God created man in His own image; in the image of God He created him; male and female He created them.

—Genesis 1:26–27

Without exception, pagan religions hold that man has disrupted and continues to disrupt nature's perfection, that man's very existence is threatening to the natural order. The Bible says that man was created by God to maintain His creation in a state of harmonious tidiness, to subdue it (Gen. 1:28) and rule over it. According to the Bible, without proper tending, nature will gradually descend into disorder and, ultimately, chaos. If you have planting areas around your home, you have been a witness to the trend toward disorder in nature—known as *entropy*. If you fail to weed and prune, those areas will be quickly overtaken by unwanted growth.

Human beings were created to be God's representatives on Earth. Theologian and best-selling author Michael Heiser uses the term

"God's imagers" to refer to our appointed role. God emphasizes our exalted status by using the word *image* three times in verses 26 and 27 of Genesis 1, the verses that describe human creation. Obviously, He feels the need to make our significance perfectly clear. Contrary to popular belief and despite the word *likeness*, the Bible never says, nor is there reason to believe, that we *look* like God. God is a spirit-being; therefore, He has no set appearance that can be described using various combinations of adjectives and nouns, as in "Bob has brown hair, a prominent nose, hazel eyes, and a moustache." (In this regard, it is interesting to note that Jesus's physical appearance is never described by the gospel writers.) Biblical phrases that refer to God creating humans in His image refer to *attributes* rather than physical characteristics.

Our status as God's imagers—His earthly representatives, charged with keeping His creation in a state of order—is certainly pertinent to the raising of—whose children? His children! All creation belongs to God! Therefore, the children about whom parents use personal pronouns—as in, "This is *our* daughter Emily" and "*My* son Henry is seven years old"–are God's children first and foremost. Human mothers and fathers are God's proxies. Using Heiser's terminology, mothers and fathers are God *imagers,* responsible for representing God to their children until they are old enough to wrap their heads around the reality of His supernatural existence.

To parent in God's image means to provide children with what God provides to the sheep in His flock: protection, provision, unconditional love, and unequivocal authority. The quintessential expression of this is found in Psalm 23:4:

> Yes, though I walk through the valley of the shadow of death,
> I will fear no evil:
> for you are with me;
> your rod and your staff they comfort me.

In the Bible, the "rod" of God is a metaphor for His all-powerful authority over all things. In effect, this very well-known scripture tells us that God's authority and His protective guidance (staff) are constant, comforting reminders of the righteousness of His discipline and love for us. Furthermore, His discipline and love are inseparable, in a perfect state of balance. That constancy and that balance constitute, therefore, the perfect parenting model, expressed in a familiar scripture:

> My son, do not despise the LORD's discipline and do not loathe
> His reproof;
> for the LORD disciplines those He loves,
> as a father the son in whom he delights.
>
> —*Proverbs 3:11–12 (BSB)*

When love dominates the love/authority equation and throws it out of balance, love is expressed as enabling and quickly develops into codependency—a state of mutual insecurity in which both parties become progressively weaker, both spiritually and emotionally. As enabling increases, authority diminishes. Furthermore, when love becomes enabling, it is no longer unconditional; rather, it becomes a bargain of mutual back-scratching in which both parties invariably begin to accuse one another of failing to scratch enough.

On the other hand, when authority dominates the love/authority equation, authority is expressed abusively—physically, verbally, emotionally, or a combination thereof. Instead of "hating" the child's inevitable misbehavior, an abusive parent acts as if he hates the *child* for misbehaving. The child, in response, begins to internalize the abuser's hate and eventually begins to hate himself. A vicious cycle quickly develops: The child's self-hate stimulates more misbehavior, which draws more hate from the abuser, which produces more self-hate, and around and around and ever downward go the abuser and the abused. That vicious cycle is simply another form of codependency, by the way.

The good news is that parents who read parenting materials of this sort are about as likely to be or become abusers of their children as pigs are to sprout wings and fly. The bad news is that since the 1960s, parental enabling (where love dominates the love/authority equation) has become epidemic, and that epidemic includes parents who read books of this sort—not all, of course, but a fair number. Please consider that I may be talking about *you*.

The problem is that enabling parents who love their children at the expense of disciplining them rarely recognize their error. They are masterful at justifying parenting behavior that effectively prevents their children from learning to take responsibility for and solve their own problems. To use a popular contemporary phrase, the parents in question *feel their children's pain*. They cannot bear to see their children suffer, even mildly, and so they attempt to solve every problem their kids experience. They don't seem to realize that suffering in a broken world such as ours cannot be avoided; it must be accepted and contended with, and the earlier in his or her life that a child learns to thus accept and thus contend, the better. It is far, far easier to learn such lessons as a child than to be forced to learn them belatedly, as an adult.

The primary characteristic of a sturdy human being is emotional resilience, the ability to stand against the hurricane, get back up if knocked down, and keep getting back up for as long as it takes to prevail or at least survive with dignity—in short, to never accept and wallow in victimhood. Emotional resilience is what enabling parents prevent their children from developing. By shielding them from life's difficulties and solving problems big and small for them, they virtually guarantee that their children's lives, as adults, will be marked by the very struggles they tried to protect them from as children. As they say, "What goes around, comes around."

FOR PERSONAL PONDERING AND GROUP DISCUSSION

1. Is your love for your child in a state of balance with your authority and discipline or is that equation out of whack? If so, in what specific way or ways?

2. Are there aspects of your parenting that are not consistent with properly serving as God's *imager* in your child's life? If so, how are you going to correct them?

3. Do you see yourself in the parent who is trying to protect his child from reality? If so, what specific things do you need to begin doing, today, to be more discerning when it comes to that protection?

7

AWARDS MEAN NADA TO GOD

These commandments that I give you today are to be on your hearts. Impress them on your children. Talk about them when you sit at home and when you walk along the road, when you lie down and when you get up.

—*Deuteronomy 6:6–7 (NIV)*

This is God's first instruction to parents. "These commandments" refers to the Ten Commandments God has just given Moses on Mount Sinai. That moral code distinguished the Israelites from all other nations and unified them into one body, with one God and one purpose.

Parents should, of course, teach the Ten Commandments to their children, but in today's America, "these commandments" refers broadly to biblical virtues and values. Even more broadly, they refer to a biblical worldview—a proper understanding of creation, God, and the redemptive work of Jesus Christ. Parents are instructed to *impress* (NIV) these concepts and comprehensions on their children, to teach them *diligently* (KJV, ESV)—words that reflect the significance of this training. With that in mind, a theologically acceptable paraphrase of the verse becomes:

You shall be persistent in teaching biblical values and an authentic biblical worldview to your children, seizing every possible opportunity to do so.

According to God, properly shaping a child's character and belief system is the utmost of parenting. It may come as a huge disappointment to some parents, but God does not care much, if at all, about a child's grades, athletic awards, or artistic accomplishments. Those are worldly concerns and goals. In and of themselves, they are not improper; nonetheless, worldly goals of that sort do not advance a child toward citizenship in God's kingdom to come. Unfortunately, however, they are the primary concerns of many of today's parents including, dare I say, many who would identify as fully committed, Bible-believing Christians.

A child's manners are a reliable gauge of whether his moral character is high on his parents' priorities. Proper instruction in social courtesies teaches a child to stop thinking about himself and pay attention to what's going on around him. Manners demonstrate respect for one's neighbor. They are also a reasonably accurate indicator of the "way" a child is "going" (Prov. 22:6). Does a child try to attract attention to himself, or does he possess a modest social demeanor? Is he humble about his achievements or a braggart? Does he appreciate and properly acknowledge what people do for him, or does he appear to feel entitled? Does he do for others without being asked? Does he interrupt adult conversations or politely wait his turn to speak? Does he possess proper table manners? That is a short list of virtues that are of lasting importance in a person's life.

When working with a small group of parents, I have them compose a ten word or phrase list describing the person they hope their child will be when he is thirty years old. Everyone comes up with pretty much the same description: respectful, responsible, trustworthy, hard-working, God-fearing, peace-loving, charitable, compassionate, humble, and service-minded. No parent has ever used descriptors referring to wealth, achievement, or prestige. Rather, they say they are trying to grow a person of good moral character. Most parents finish the list in less than five minutes. Very few parents, however, manage to finish the next part of the exercise without some difficulty: "Write down one thing," I ask, "you've done in the last week for the specific, intentional purpose of strengthening one of the character attributes you just listed."

Let's face it, most parents put lots of energy on a weekly basis into helping their children achieve academically, athletically, and artistically—much more energy than they put into strengthening manners and morals. The parents in question are dutiful about helping their kids with their homework and study for tests. They drive them from one activity to another in labored pursuit of accomplishment and self-esteem. Some even hire personal coaches for their kids, hoping they will someday win scholarships of one sort or another. And on it goes. In short, their day-to-day parenting practice does not align with what they would say they want to accomplish. When the parents in question are Christian, that "say one thing and do another" disconnect explains why their parenting struggles are no different than those reported to me by secular parents.

Do the same thing, have the same problems.

FOR PERSONAL PONDERING AND GROUP DISCUSSION

1. If you have not already done so, write ten words or phrases you hope will describe your child when he or she is thirty years old. Then, for each item on your list, identify something you have done in the last week or so with the specific intention of strengthening it.

2. What does the above exercise reveal about your parenting priorities? Are they consistent with a full commitment to biblical values and principles? How can you bring your stated priorities and your day-to-day parenting practices into better alignment?

3. Are your child's social manners high on your list of parenting priorities? How could you do a better job of strengthening them?

8

THE SEASONS OF
PARENTHOOD

There is a time for everything and a season for every activity
under the heavens.

—Ecclesiastes 3:1 (NIV)

The words "everything" and "every" in this familiar scripture are all-in-
clusive, meaning that as is the case with growing crops, growing children
is governed by seasons both specific and general. There is a season for
toilet training, for example (eighteen to twenty-four months), during
which a child readily learns what is required. Parents who let that season
come and go are likely to have great difficulty convincing a child of,
say, three, to cooperate in what is long overdue. But in addition to there
being optimal windows of time for introducing new skills to a child,
the entirety of child-rearing is divided into major seasons, each of which
requires that parents play a distinct role. Child-rearing's seasons—of
which there are three—are part of God's design for human beings;
therefore, they cannot be altered. Parents either conform their behavior
to the requirements of each season, or they do not.

The first of these, which I call the Season of Service, begins when a
child is born and lasts for approximately two years during which parents
serve, in the most basic of ways, a child who cannot serve himself and is

not able to anticipate the consequences of his actions. His dependency and unknowing require that his parents place him at the center of their attention and orbit around him in a near-constant ministry of surveillance and "doing"—feeding, carrying, changing, comforting, fixing, fetching, and so on. The purposes of Season 1 are threefold:

- "Root" the child securely in the world—assure him that he is where he belongs, with people who cherish him.
- Provide for the child's fundamental biological needs—food, water, and shelter.
- Prevent the child from hurting himself.

In all cultures and in all times, the mother has been the primary servant during Season 1. The father stands slightly outside the periphery of his wife's busy orbit, functioning as her "parenting aide." Like a teacher's aide is to a teacher, the father's job during these first two years or so is to assist his wife and fill in for her when she needs a break. Consequent to this child-centeredness, the marriage is "catch-as-catch-can" during Season 1. The fact that he is the center of attention, that the "world" revolves around him, does not escape the youngster in question. He may lack language skills, but he is highly intelligent and intuitive. He is drawing inarticulate conclusions concerning how things work in his world, one of which is that his mother is there to do his bidding. He verifies this by crying, at which his mother appears and does everything in her power to fix whatever is causing his distress, thus confirming in the child's mind that she is his personal fetcher and fixer.

The pre-modern mother understood that whereas what she was doing for her child during Season 1 was necessary, she was slowly creating a monster. If she did not bring Season 1 to a close, she was in danger of raising a spoiled brat—a child who would believe that as his mother was doing, the world revolved around him. And so, around her child's second birthday, that old-fashioned mom set about to correct his initial impression of what she represented in his life. Under normal circumstances, this course correction takes about a year. It is, without question, the most significant and precedent-setting of all times in the parent–child relationship. To bring about this transformation, a mother must accomplish three things:

- Teach and expect her child to do for himself a fair amount of what she has previously done for him—use the toilet instead of diapers, get himself a drink and basic snacks, dress himself, pick up his toys, and so on. There will be times, of course, when Mom will still have to serve; but whereas service is the rule in Season 1, it should be the exception from that time forward.

- Establish a boundary between herself and her child, thus limiting his access to her—make him wait before she does something for him, instruct him to go elsewhere while she finishes a task, and so on.

- Back slowly out of a state of high involvement with her child and reestablish the marriage as the family's relationship of prominence.

As is so often the case when seasons change, this transitional year is marked by storms of protest from a child who wants Season 1 to go on forever. Who can blame him? Who would not want a servant for life? But if the mother stays the course, then by the time her child is three, he will see her with new eyes—once a servant, now a formidable authority figure who is not to be trifled with. Once at the center of Mom's world, Mom and Dad are now the center of his. They insist that he do more and more things for himself, give them "space" to do what they need and want to do (including putting their feet up and doing nothing), and Mom begins making it perfectly clear that her relationship with his father trumps her relationship with him.

The transition between Seasons 1 and 2 of parenthood takes about a year. If the child's parents are focused and purposeful during this transition, Season 2, the Season of Leadership and Authority, begins around the child's third birthday and lasts ten years, until age thirteen. The parents' job during Season 2, which I also call the Decade of Discipline, is to provide their child with effective *government*. Their new purpose is to govern such that their child (a) consents to their government (becomes their willing disciple), and (b) internalizes their discipline and gradually develops the self-restraint necessary to govern himself responsibly.

Around age thirteen, a second transition takes place (or should) that moves parent and child into Season 3, the Season of Mentoring. It is no coincidence that in traditional cultures, early adolescent rites of passage—the Jewish bar mitzvah and bat mitzvah being surviving examples—occur when a child is thirteen. These rituals mark and celebrate a major transition in the parent–child relationship. They acknowledge that the child in question has completed the disciplinary "curriculum" of Season 2 and is now regarded as self-governing. He no longer needs adults to define right and wrong for him; rather, he needs adult mentors to help him acquire the practical skills he will need to emancipate successfully—how to apply for a job, balance a budget, and so on.

Within the framework of this seasonal approach to parenting, children generally emancipate relatively early. As recently as 1970, the average age of successful emancipation (i.e., full economic and residential independence) was twenty. But then these were young people who were born around 1950, before child-rearing common sense and intuition were overwhelmed by an avalanche of psychobabble. Since then, the average age of successful emancipation has risen to twenty-seven. Something is obviously wrong.

Season	Age of Child	Parent Role	Parenting Goal
1 Service	Birth–2	Servant	Secure child
2 Leadership	3–13	Authority	Self-governing child
3 Mentoring	13–emancipation	Mentor	Emancipated child

These days, child rearing is rarely taking place in accord with its natural seasons, and it has not been since the 1960s. The culture-wide symptoms include late emancipation and boomerang children as well as younger children who are disrespectful, self-destructive, depressed, irresponsible, and exhibit toddler behavior (short attention span, impulsivity, low tolerance for frustration, inability to delay gratification, tantrums, belligerent defiance) well beyond chronological toddlerhood.

The breakdown is occurring between the second and third birthdays, when it is imperative that a mother initiate the transition between Seasons 1 and 2 and then team with her husband and complete it. This all-important transition took place rather reliably fifty and more years ago; it takes place rarely today. The mother of fifty-plus years ago had permission from the culture—including friends, extended family, and other mothers—to bring about this change in her child's life. Today's mother does not.

All too often, by the time her child is three years old, today's mom is often found trapped in the Good Mommy Club (GMC), a tacit sisterhood that exerts tremendous pressure on its members to conform to standards that lock women into Season 1 in perpetuity. According to GMC standards, the Good Mommy pays as much attention to her child as she is able, does as much for her child as she is able, and solves all her child's problems—regardless of her child's age. The Good Mommy is a servant not for two years, but forever. In effect, even if she is married, she thinks of herself as a single parent. In her mind, the success of her child-rearing project or projects will be a matter of *her* dedication, *her* devotion, and *her* diligent doing. She has been brainwashed to think that constant child-oriented busyness is the measure of a Good Mommy; therefore, she is unable to exercise effective authority over her child.

The principles of leadership are unchanged from one leadership context to another. In whatever arena they are found, effective leaders:

- Have no problem making unpopular decisions and staying the course.
- Delegate responsibility.
- Establish a boundary between themselves and those they lead. The boundary is permeable, but the leader controls its permeability.

If a corporate CEO does not abide by the above principles, he will fail to convey authority effectively. The same is true of a parent. Unfortunately, Good Mommy Club doctrine paralyzes a mother's ability to make decisions that cause her child distress. A servant, after all, is supposed to please and be pleasing. If today's mother makes a decision that upsets her child, she is likely to interpret her child's angst as indication that she has made the wrong decision and reverse her course. The new standards virtually require a mother to be a micromanager, perpetually scurrying from one task to another, making sure everything is going as it should.

Once upon a time not so long ago, children performed chores at the direction of their mothers. Today's mother believes that the more a mother does on behalf of her child, regardless of the child's age, the better a mother she is. And so, even today's typical seven-year-old child is virtually chore-free. He's on a never-ending welfare plan.

The new standard also denies a mother permission to establish a boundary between herself and her child. It says that a Good Mommy is highly involved with her child, and the more highly involved, the better. Under the circumstances, it is forbidden for today's mom to ever, under any circumstances, deny her child access to her. If he wants her attention, she is to drop what she is doing and give it. She is even to sleep with her child if he demands it! My mother, typical of her generation, had no problem shooing me out from underfoot, telling me I had no permission to be in the same room with her when she was doing something that required her undivided attention and warning me that if I did not find something to do and leave her alone, she would find something for me to do. Today's mom is thrown for a loop at the thought of telling her child that something she is doing is more important than something he wants her to do. She lives in fear of doing something that might disturb her child in the least, believing that any such disturbance might translate into apocalyptic damage to his self-esteem. He might begin to feel unworthy, unwanted, and unloved. That's absurd, but even in that event, so what? Children are drama factories. So what if a child who is loved unconditionally thinks that his mother speaking sternly to him means he is not loved? That changes nothing! Should he begin crying and blurt, "You don't love me anymore!" his mother's proper response is, "That's ridiculous, and I'm not going to stop what I'm doing and attend your pity-party."

I vividly remember my mother saying to me, "John Rosemond, you don't need a mother right now, and I'm not going to be one. Now, stop bothering me and go find something to do." She said it calmly and matter-of-factly; therefore, I knew she was serious. It is the rare mother today who can bring herself to say something equivalent to "You don't need a mother right now, and I'm not going to be one," much less "You're bothering me." The psychobabblers have convinced today's mom that speech of that sort will cause her child psychological disruption, generate an "attachment disorder" or "bonding issues," cause him to question her commitment to him, send his self-esteem into a tailspin, or all the above. They have successfully implanted in her head a swarm of what I call "psychological boogeymen" who cause her to be constantly afraid that one wrong step in her parenting will shatter her child's supposedly fragile psyche. Under the circumstances, it is impossible for her to assert a calm, matter-of-fact authority. So, she fails in her leadership. She is caught in a conundrum: On the one hand, she is expected to be highly involved and in great relationship with her child, and on the other to discipline him properly. These two expectations cancel each other. So, today's mother is frustrated in her attempts to discipline and thus experiences more discipline problems than her grandmother even thought possible.

The great paradox of modern parenting is that women have claimed authority in every area of life except where their children are concerned. As a result, their kids are growing up without respect for female authority—a sorry state of affairs that bodes ill for everyone.

FOR PERSONAL PONDERING AND GROUP DISCUSSION

1. Did you enter Season 2 with your child around his third birthday— on schedule, in other words—or were you still stuck in Season 1? If the latter, what specific steps can you take, beginning today, to bring your parenting back into alignment with God's seasonal design?
2. If you are determined to move beyond Season 1 and put your child in his or her proper place, how do you intend to deal with opposition from your child? How, for example, will you deal with his tantrums at discovering that you will no longer perform as he commands?
3. This week, add, "You don't need a mother right now, and I am not going to be one" to your parenting vocabulary. How does it feel? How does your child feel about it? So what?

9
THE FIRST PARENTING COMMANDMENT

And one of them, a lawyer, asked him a question to test him.
"Teacher, which is the great commandment in the Law?" And
he said to him, "You shall love the Lord your God with all your
heart and with all your soul and with all your mind. This is the
great and first commandment."

—*Matthew 22:35–39*

In his Gospel, the apostle Matthew recounts a scene in which a Pharisee,
seeking to make Jesus stumble and be exposed as a charlatan, asks Him
to identify the "great commandment in the Law." The fellow does not
know that he is asking the question of none other than the very Author
of the Law. Jesus may have smiled, if inwardly, at the man's naivete.
He tells His interrogator that the commandment in question is, "You
shall love the Lord your God with all your heart and with all your soul
and with all your mind." In everything that we do as Christians, that
"great and first" commandment should be foremost in our thinking,
foremost to our purpose. There is no exception, no caveat, to that truism.
God Himself has said so. Putting love of God utmost in our lives and
in everything we do is the very essence of a biblical worldview. The

question, then, becomes: How does the Great and First Commandment pertain to the rearing of children?

Many—perhaps the majority—of parents who come to hear me speak on what Americans now call "parenting" are hoping I will address specific discipline problems they are experiencing with their kids. The problems in question run the gamut—tantrums, disobedience, disrespect, underperformance in school, and so on. These parents are anticipating that I will recommend a disciplinary method—what I sometimes call a "consequence delivery system."

But I do not address the issue of discipline primarily in terms of methods. I even say, "You have already learned that methods alone won't solve your discipline problems—you simply aren't accepting the evidence. That's why you keep trying one method after another, to no avail. The secret to proper discipline is not proper methods; it is a proper point of view, a proper attitude. That is what you're lacking, and that is what you need. Furthermore, it's what your kids need from you."

I am referring to what I call a proper *parent-view*. As the term implies, a proper parent-view is the parenting equivalent of a proper worldview. Evangelical Christians know (or should) that a proper worldview—informed by the Word of God—is essential to living a proper Christian life—which is to say, a proper life. Likewise, a proper parent-view is informed by the Word of God and is essential to right and proper child-rearing. What I am about to say is bound to startle some folks, but in the context of a proper, biblical parent-view, a parent's first and foremost obligation is not to his or her child; it is, rather, to God. As you will discover in the next chapter, one's child does not even come second! A parent's first obligation is to demonstrate, through his or her child-rearing, unmitigated love of and obedience toward God. That is essentially what Paul meant when he exhorted fathers to raise their children "in the training and instruction of the Lord" (Ephesians 6:4, chapter 15). Ironically, by putting obligation to God in front of obligation to their children, parents will do a much better job. The fact is you cannot do a proper job at anything without first putting your priorities in proper order.

Parents use personal pronouns when referring to their children. They use phrases like "my child" and "our children" when in fact their children are, first and foremost, God's children. The following analogy is apt: Just as a nanny's first obligation is to the parents of a child in her care, a parent's first obligation in the raising of a child is to our heavenly Parent. Like a nanny is a proxy, so too is a parent. Parents execute this obligation by putting what God wants of them in front of what the world expects and encourages and most certainly in front of what their children want from them. In the raising of children, parents honor God by doing two things: first, following His instructions; second, properly acting as His proxies, His stand-ins. Parents are to model God to their children. They are to act like superior beings whose love is unconditional and whose authority is indisputable.

God's instructions to parents are quite simple. He instructs parents to put their marriages first and foremost in their families (Gen. 2:24), to instruct their children in a biblical worldview (Deut. 6:6–7), to compel their children to control their emotions (Prov. 22:15), and to "aim" their parenting at a vision of the God-fearing adults they want their children to become (Prov. 22:6). It could be argued that these four scriptures provide parents with direction sufficient to doing a good job.

As I say as often as the opportunity presents itself, God does not really care what a child's grades are, He does not care that a child accumulates numerous athletic awards, and He does not care that a child becomes president of the United States. He cares that a child's character and worldview conform to His standards. That is the alpha and omega of parenting.

FOR PERSONAL PONDERING AND GROUP DISCUSSION

1. What could you do as a parent to better demonstrate your love of God in how you raise your kids?
2. How do you think your children would react if you "demoted" them in terms of your parenting priorities? If they reacted negatively, would that cause you insecurity? Would their negative reaction cause you to question your decision? If so, why?
3. What makes it difficult for even the most committed Christian to put God first in everything they do?

10
THE SECOND PARENTING COMMANDMENT

"And a second is like it: You shall love your neighbor as yourself."

—Matthew 22:40

I am a member of the last generation of American children who were not Big Deals. As was the case with every generation of parents before them, the so-called Greatest Generation kept us—their children—in proper perspective. My mother, for example, told me in so many words and on more than several occasions that her purpose was not to raise a straight A student—my academic achievement was my responsibility, not hers—but to raise a good citizen, meaning a person who was respectful of others no matter their circumstances, compassionate, charitable, hard-working, trustworthy, and always put forth his best effort. As Mom often reminded me, the world did not revolve because of or around me. My mother, a single parent for much of my first seven years, felt that in raising me, her obligation to her neighbors, broadly defined, overrode her obligation to me. Mind you, she loved me dearly. I never doubted that. But when I look back on my childhood, it is obvious that my character—how a person treats other people—was uppermost in her mind.

Perhaps my mother's example is why, when I am speaking to a group of people, I always say, "Proper parenting is an act of love for one's neighbors." Conversely, inflicting an ill-mannered child on other people, including teachers and coaches, is an act of disrespect. It is discourteous for parents to bring an inadequately disciplined child into a fine dining restaurant, someone else's home, an orchestral concert, or just about anywhere public, in fact.

Granted, the proper discipline of a child is of great benefit to the child, but it can be argued that the greatest benefit is to one's neighbors. You teach your child to share for the benefit of other children. You teach your child to obey legitimate adult authority for the benefit of his teachers, coaches, and his friend's parents. You teach your child to be truthful and trustworthy for the benefit of everyone with whom he will ever have relationship. You teach your child to be hard-working for the benefit of his future employers and co-workers. You teach your child the value of serving others for the benefit of everyone, but especially for his or her future spouse.

Putting your child-rearing obligation to your neighbors next in line behind your obligation to God requires that you begin making new habits. Establishing a new habit involves keeping it in the forefront of your thinking and practicing it until it becomes second nature. Make sticky notes to yourself that read REMEMBER, MY PRIMARY PARENTING OBLIGATIONS ARE TO GOD AND NEIGHBOR! and put them in strategic places around your home. In challenging child-rearing situations, practice asking yourself, "How should I handle this in a manner that best reflects my new parenting priorities?" In no time at all, you will be a "born-again" parent with a new sense of direction and purpose!

Here is the paradox: Putting obligation to children third, behind obligation to God and obligation to neighbors, imparts untold benefit to said children. First, that arrangement helps children put themselves in proper perspective. The earlier a child understands that the world does not turn because of him or for his personal benefit, the better. That understanding is the essence of humility, and humility is the biblical ideal (not self-esteem). Second, that arrangement helps children understand that their own priorities should be to God and neighbor.

Because their parents put obligation to God and neighbor in front of obligation to them, those kids will be better people and will live far more satisfying lives.

FOR PERSONAL PONDERING AND GROUP DISCUSSION

1. In what concrete, practical ways can you make love of your neighbors a greater priority in your parenting?

2. Think of a situation involving your children, recent or otherwise, that you would have handled differently had you acted primarily in terms of obligation to (love of) neighbor.

3. How will your neighbors, broadly speaking, react to you putting obligation to them in front of obligation to your kids? Will they be mystified? Will they be concerned? Will they think you've gone "off the rails"? Or, will they be grateful? How will you deal with their reactions?

11
PARENT WITH VISION!

Train up a child in the way he should go, and when he is old he will not depart from it.

—Proverbs 22:6

Of all Bible verses that speak directly to the raising of children, Proverbs 22:6 is certainly the most well-known. God instructs parents to raise a child in keeping with the "way he should go"—that is, consistent with a vision of the child in question as a God-fearing, responsible adult who is both a good citizen of the culture and a future citizen of God's kingdom.

Note that "way" is singular, referring to the fact that there is God's *one* right way to raise a child and a host of wrong ways. Those postmodern contrivances include attachment parenting, free-range parenting, shame-free parenting, democratic parenting, grace-based parenting, indigo parenting, and the many other variations on "parenting" that have arisen since the late 1960s. As the astute reader may have noticed, the parenting Tower of Babble even includes iterations that are supposedly drawn from scripture but are in fact more psychological than biblical in nature. God's one right way to raise children does not need a fancy name. It is simply God's one right way, *His perfect parenting plan.*

As the Bible makes clear, the right path is always narrow (Matt. 7:14, chapter 30). Staying on a narrow pathway requires concentration, vigilance, steadfastness. It requires that one be able, concerning any given issue or task and at any given moment in time, to discriminate between what the world wants of us, what we want for ourselves, and what God wants of us.

The first two of those options—what the world wants of us and what we desire for ourselves—are the human defaults. They represent pathways that bring social approval, influence, instant gratification, wealth, and every other prideful thing. Every default pathway leads to destruction. Satan is the "prince of this world" (John 14:30), and he always, without exception, wants us to do the very opposite of what God wants us to do. Satan is akin to one of the sirens of ancient Greek mythology, always enticing us to listen to and gravitate toward him instead of God (and as with the sirens, to gravitate toward Satan is to wind up floundering on metaphorical rocks).

Satan uses appeals to hedonism and pride—pleasure, prestige, possessions—to manipulate people. He also uses children because nothing sways a parent more effectively and reliably than matters concerning his or her children. As many parents admit, "I'll do anything for my kids." Satan manipulates parents into lying for their children, breaking the law for their children, going into debilitating debt for their children, giving their kids smart phones, buying their kids expensive cars on their sixteenth birthdays, letting unemployed adult children live in their basements playing video games, and other equally immoral and downright dumb "anythings." Do not ever say you are willing to do anything for your kids. The kids in question have permission to never truly grow up. Everyone needs to know there is a limit on what will be condoned and supported.

The world places value on the accomplishments of children, and that is what distracts and even consumes many parents. Supporting a child who wants to accomplish a certain thing is fine until that support becomes an obsession and the child's accomplishment becomes an idol. When God says to raise a child in the "way he should go," the way of worldly success is not what He means. What "way" should a child be trained to? The way of the Lord, of course!

How can you go about training your child to walk in the way of Christ? Five actions are critical:

1. Walking in the way of Christ yourself (being a proper role model).
2. Diligently teaching God's moral law (Deut. 6:6–7).
3. Regular Bible study that includes and is sometimes even directed primarily at your child (equipping a child with the armor of God).
4. Teaching your child to pray (another means of equipping a child with God's armor).
5. Participating as a family in a church community (fellowship with like-minded Christians).

If a child demonstrates talent in a certain area, parents should be encouraging, but never should supporting a child's talents eclipse the responsibility of impressing a biblical worldview upon the child. All too many contemporary parents are distracted by their children's achievements and a desire to have "wonderful relationships" with their children. That is Satan at work, trying to divert parents from their foremost responsibilities to God and neighbor.

Satan's most effective and relentless attacks on the Body of Christ are directed at Jesus's Church and the Christian family. He divides congregations over the most trivial of concerns, like whether God should be worshipped with hymns or praise music. Likewise, he does all he can to disrupt the family and undermine its true, godly purpose. In a very real sense, whenever two or three are gathered in Christ's name (Matt. 18:20), Satan or one of his posse of demons is always lurking nearby. Four facts that Christian parents should keep in mind as they train their children up in the way they should go:

1. Satan does not want parents to succeed at raising children who choose Christ. He wants parents to raise children who think Christ is a myth, a joke, or both.
2. When it comes to raising a child who eventually chooses Christ, being a Christian parent will prove advantageous, but being Christian does not guarantee that outcome or even a reasonably good one. Bad things can and do sometimes happen to good people.
3. Raising a child who chooses Christ requires that parents put on the armor of God (obtained through prayer and working knowledge of His Word) and engage in spiritual warfare on the child's behalf.

4. The spiritual warfare in question requires training and instruction in the way the child should go.

Proverbs 22:6 is, in effect, a call to action on the part of parents. It says to parents that if they want their children to follow Christ and live godly lives, they must leave nothing to chance. In this regard, parents must do three things:

1. *Train*. They must be focused, intentional, strategic, and vigilant.
2. **Train *up***. They must be clear that their job is to lift their children out of bondage to sin—lives that are me-centric—and into lives that are Christ-centric.
3. **Train to the one right *way*.** The way in question is God's narrow path. Parents must possess a clear vision of the adult they are raising and "aim" their parenting at that vision every day, in every parenting situation, like an archer aims at a bullseye.

Discipline is the process by which parents, as God's proxies, transform the antisocial, "me first!" toddler (actually, most children at that stage are "me *only!*") into a prosocial adult who loves God and loves his neighbor. The successful discipling of a child will, at times, necessitate correction and punishment, but its most fundamental ingredient is conscientious instruction as referred to in Deuteronomy where parents are commanded to *impress* godly values on their children with *diligence* (6:7 in NIV and ESV, respectively). That is the heart of the training to which this scripture refers. It is training in one way and one way only.

Proverbs 22:6 has a fly in its ointment: *"and when he is old, he will not depart from it."* Some parents interpret the verse as an assurance that proper training in biblical values will unfailingly produce a fine, upstanding adult who chooses Christ. But parenting is not deterministic. Children—all children—do things at times that are completely unrelated to anything their parents have or have not done. Plus, children are by nature sinful. They sin regardless of their upbringings. Combine human free will with a child's sin nature, and one has the potential for many troubles. Consider that the only perfect Parent there ever was or will be created two children who committed egregious sin the moment His back was turned!

Everyone knows of good, moral parents whose kids went off the proverbial deep end and never came back. Likewise, everyone knows of good, moral adults whose upbringing was defined by one adversity after another—drug-addled parents, abuse, abandonment, foster home after foster home, and so on. Parenting is certainly an *influence* on how a child turns out; arguably, the most significant influence of all. Nonetheless, there is no reliable cause-and-effect relationship. Another way of saying the same thing: A child is going to be influenced by things over which his parents have little to no control. Plus, as I recall my grandmother saying, "Every child has a mind of his own." Every child possesses free will, and their choices sometimes boggle the mind. (For an optimistic take on this, read the story of the prodigal son in Luke 15:11–32).

But psychology is the reigning secular religion of our time, and parenting determinism is part and parcel of a psychological belief system. Most folks, therefore, believe parenting produces the person, that the behavior of a child's parents reliably predicts the behavior of the child when he or she is an adult. This erroneous belief, in combination with the idea that Proverbs 22:6 is a promise, causes lots of grief. The grief in question is almost always expressed thus: "What did we do wrong to raise a child who _____ (fill in the blank with some dysfunctionality or immorality)?" To the parents in question, their adult child's problems are evidence they failed miserably. After all, they reason, if training a child in the "way he should go" results in an adult child who does not "depart from it," then an adult child who has strayed far from the right path must be evidence that his parents did not train properly. That misinterpretation of the verse leads some parents into a swamp of guilt, perpetual regret, and ongoing self-recrimination.

Proverbs 22:6 is a *principle,* not a promise. In other words, it does not say that if parents do A, then their child will surely do B; but it does say that if parents do A, B is the *most likely* outcome to the child. If, for example, parents are conscientious but not overbearing and legalistic in biblical instruction to a child, the child is likely to adopt their faith as an adult—but no one can guarantee that outcome.

Proverbs 22:6 may also be thought of as a caution, one that is particularly relevant to Christian parents who are trying to navigate a culture chock full of worldly attractions like smart phones and other devices that will connect a child, in a heartbeat, to things they are not ready to encounter—intellectually, spiritually, morally, or emotionally.

Children do not know what they *need*; they only know what they *want*, and they want what feels good, tastes good, looks good, sounds good—in other words, they want what excites their senses and evokes pride, which is why children are so prone to complaining that life is "boring." The Bible is clear that we—every single human being past, present, and future—is in desperate need of Christ because we are born dead in trespasses and sins (Eph. 2:1–3). In short, everyone begins his or her life with a moral handicap. The last thing one wants to do is encourage in children what is naturally found in their hearts—pragmatic self-centeredness, a "me first" attitude. But humanism, the world's default philosophy, sets parents to the task of doing exactly that. The online edition of the Merriam-Webster Dictionary defines humanism as a worldview that "rejects the supernatural," stressing instead the inherent worth of the individual and capacity for something called "self-realization through reason." In effect, humanism embraces and promotes the notion that human beings can transcend material limitations and evolve into quasi-divine beings (as in the serpent's promise to Eve that by eating of the tree of knowledge, she could become "like God"). Humanism is reflected in parent speech of this sort:

- "It's been difficult and still is at times, but I've learned to adjust my parenting to Billy's need to feel that he's in control of his own life."
- "Lucy doesn't respond well to firm authority, so I persuaded the principal to put her with a younger teacher who is flexible, tolerant, and patient."
- "I don't want Susie to be the only child in her peer group, who doesn't have something all the other kids have. The teenage years are hard enough without parents who force you to be different."
- "Johnny is a very sensitive child who needs lots of positive attention and verbal affirmation."
- "I've come to realize that if I'm going to parent Ellie in a way that comes alongside her journey toward self-actualization, where we're walking together in the same direction, I need to first discover who she is and is not."

That sort of parent-speak reflects an approach to the raising of children that is more influenced by psychology and the world than God's Word. Psychology has caused many parents, out of concern for their children's self-esteem (which psychology and the world say they should possess in abundance, while the Bible says they should not possess at all), to make idols of their children. Idols cloud a person's thought processes. A person who creates an idol cannot view the idol with any degree of objectivity. A person who has made an idol of a sports team, for example, may become incensed if someone criticizes the team or any of its members or the team loses a game because of a supposedly "bad call." Likewise, a parent who has made an idol of his or her child is unable to see the child objectively. In both cases, the idol can do no wrong. Child-idolatry is why so many teachers testify that when they report misbehavior, parents often become defensive, even angry, and deny that their children are even remotely capable of the wrongdoings in question. Along those same lines, a Southern Baptist pastor once told me that while every parent in his congregation would agree with the statement "I am a sinner," very few would agree with the statement "My *child* is a sinner."

As I have already pointed out, training up a child in keeping with God's will emphasizes character over accomplishment. It cannot be over-emphasized: God does not place much if any value on a child's worldly achievements. Those are worldly "treasures" of the sort referred to in Matthew 6:19. God cares that a child turns out to be a person of integrity and has unwavering faith in His Son. Worldly accomplishments are like man's monuments; eventually, they crumble into dust. A godly character endures eternally. No one will be allowed to bring the things they acquired on earth—titles, honors, expensive cars, jewelry, vacation homes—with them into heaven (see Matt. 6:19–21).

In the Christian community, one huge and growing problem is parents who don't know what they should be doing. Most of those parents, however, are teachable. They can be steered toward the right path. The much bigger problem is parents who know what they should be doing and are not doing it. Instead, they are allowing themselves to be caught up in worldly expectations. No doubt about it, swimming against a worldly tide is difficult and even dispiriting at times. Its reward is certainly not immediate. For that very reason, it requires fortitude, forbearance, perseverance, and eyes that are fixed firmly on the future, on the prize that awaits.

Along this same vein, teachers unanimously testify that the best students are not necessarily those with the highest IQs, but those who are most respectful, responsible, and obedient. As my grandmother—a repository of parenting wisdom—used to say, "A high IQ and ten cents will get you a cup of coffee." (Yes, Virginia, there was a time when a cup of coffee cost ten cents!) In the classroom as in life, intelligence takes a back seat to such traits as persistence, integrity, trustworthiness, modesty, and humility. Moms and dads have approximately eighteen years to develop kids into men and women who serve God and love Christ. Everything else is window dressing.

FOR PERSONAL PONDERING AND GROUP DISCUSSION

1. Do you intend to make alterations to your parenting approach in response to this chapter? If so, what and how?
2. What are the biggest challenges to implementing and staying the course with a biblical approach to rearing children? How can you overcome those challenges?
3. What are the ways in which you are intentionally training or preparing your child for adulthood? Is your focus primarily on character development or on such things as your child's achievements in school and extra-curricular activities? Which are easier to promote? Which are more important in the long run?

12

THE CONGENITAL
STATE OF THE HEART

Foolishness is bound in the heart of a child...
—*Proverbs 22:15 (NASB)*

It is logically impossible for a child, even a young teen, to be clear on what is and is not in his or her own best interest. Experience across a relatively broad array of matters along with a willingness to accept full responsibility for everything you do and everything that happens to you is necessary to knowing what is in your own best interests. That mental, emotional, and spiritual condition is known as adulthood.

Unfortunately, some parents seem to think that even young children know what is best for themselves. An example: A mother refuses her five-year-old's demand to be allowed a sleepover at a friend's home. Said child begins to cry piteously, throws herself to the floor, and proceeds to act, by adult standards, insane. The child's highly emotional reaction throws her mother off balance. She begins second-guessing herself. She interprets her child's meltdown as indication that she may have made the wrong decision. Unsure of herself, she begins to back-peddle, to search for a compromise that her daughter will accept. She eventually comes up with one, and sure enough, Her Majesty is happy again—until next time, that is. The mom in question:

- believes, in effect, that her primary job is that of raising a "happy" child; therefore, when her daughter becomes unhappy, she believes it is her responsibility to do whatever is necessary to restore her happiness.
- does not know that children are clueless concerning the difference between what is and what is not in their best interests.
- is unwittingly giving her daughter power over her, which said daughter expresses as lunatic emotional outbursts.
- instead of acting to "drive" the foolishness of her child's heart "far from her" through firm demonstration of her authority (see next chapter), she enables her daughter's emotionality.

Make no mistake about it, the "foolishness" referred to in Proverbs 22:15 is one and the same with a child's sin nature. Take note that a child's sin nature is "bound" in her heart, meaning that her heart is a virtual prisoner to irrationality and emotionality. Quite a few Bible verses refer to the heart's inclination toward evil, including:

- "The heart is more deceitful than all else, and is desperately sick; who can understand it?" (Jer. 17:9)
- "The LORD smelled the soothing aroma; and the LORD said to Himself, 'I will never again curse the ground on account of man, for the intent of man's heart is evil from his youth.'" (Gen. 8:21)
- "But the things that proceed out of the mouth come from the heart, and those defile the man. 'For out of the heart come evil thoughts, murders, adulteries, fornications, thefts, false witness, slanders.'" (Matt. 15:18–19)

Some people, unfortunately, never manage to free themselves from a state of bondage to their emotions. Everyone knows at least one adult who fits that description. The people in question have never grown up. Their emotions rule their behavior. Discipline is the process by which a child is forced to grow up—become productive, self-supporting, and accepting of full responsibility for his life. Yes, *forced*. Human beings begin their lives in a completely dependent, irresponsible state and struggle for the whole of their lives with wanting to restore that state of counterfeit bliss. Growing up must be forced and enforced until the individual in question begins to understand that obedience and responsibility are necessary to personal well-being.

Obedient people are happy people. Common sense confirms that, but so has social science research. The world, dominated by the dark prince and his minions, wants you to believe that happiness is all about wealth, power, prestige, and acquisition. Not so. Taking yours truly as an example, I am immeasurably happier—content and full of hope— today that I ever imagined was possible before I chose to obey Him and knocked on His door. The new parenting experts, however, claimed that obedience is a bad thing. They claimed—as usual, without a shred of objective evidence—that obedient children were fearful and unable to think for themselves. They frequently used the word *robots*. Having set up a straw man, they proceeded to knock it down and almost out. Once Boomer parents fell under the sway of this myth, they were enticed to eat, once again, from the tree of knowledge. This time, the fruit was bursting with psychological parenting toxins.

As the new ideas dug deeper and deeper into the collective parenting mind-set, mother–child codependency became the norm, fathers abandoned their true and rightful responsibilities as heads of their families, the typical family became a *de facto* matriarchy, and parents began catering to and even obeying their children. As is obvious to folks in my generation—most of whom, as children, experienced authentic childhood—the problem has nothing to do with children. With rare exception, a child will eventually submit to being disciplined if the discipline is righteous. The problem is parents who recoil at the notion that discipline requires *force* and choke on the word *obedience*. So, parents now call obedience by a new name: *cooperation*. The new name sounds nicer, but cooperation is only possible between equals. Parental attempts to coax *cooperation* from a child usually result in the child becoming a tyrant. Children either obey, or they do not obey. *Cooperation* is not in their wheelhouse. Their minds have not matured to a point of being able to wrap their heads around the complex nature of negotiation, and the ability to cooperate cannot exist without the ability to negotiate fairly.

Because discipline is rarely forceful any longer—calm, composed, and compelling—the foolishness bound in the hearts of children is not being dislodged and driven away. In addition, boys are being demonized and feminized, and girls are becoming sexualized and addicted to drama. The canaries in the coal mine are the ongoing deterioration of child and teen mental health and the rising age of successful emancipation. In 1982, author/educator Neil Postman predicted *The Disappearance of Childhood* (Delacorte Press, 1982), but what we now have on our collective hands is an epidemic of never-ending childhood. But whether childhood is disappearing or never-ending, it is all the same. When childhood never ends, it ceases to exist as a temporary condition and simply becomes the way things are in perpetuity.

The facts scream, "Parents! Wake up to your responsibilities to God and neighbor! You're falling asleep at the wheel! You're letting pride drive how you raise your kids!"

The bottom line: Foolishness cannot drive foolishness out of someone else's heart.

FOR PERSONAL PONDERING AND GROUP DISCUSSION

1. Have you been a "foolish" parent? Have you followed the world's parenting path? Has your parenting goal been that of promoting your child's happiness and success, and have you, in turn, failed at driving foolishness from your child's heart? If so, are you ready and willing to begin the process of recovery? What first step will you take?

2. Explain how cooperation depends on the ability of all parties to negotiate with respect for one another. Then, explain why children are incapable of cooperation.

3. When foolishness is driven from a child's heart, it creates a vacuum that is meant to be filled by desirable attributes. What are they? How are they essential to authentic adulthood?

13
THE ROD

… but the rod of discipline will drive it far from him.

—*Proverbs 22:15*

You may have noticed, but in case you did not, I have separated Proverbs 22:15 into two parts and devoted a chapter to each, the reason being that the first and second "halves" of the verse raise distinct issues. In the case of the second half, the word *rod* has been the subject of an unfortunate interpretation that begs for correction. Of primary concern is the idea that "the rod" refers to spankings along with the belief that God commands parents to spank liberally.

On occasion, folks have informed me that the Bible warns of spanking too little. "Remember," they say. "Spare the rod, spoil the child." The truth is, however, that just as the Constitution of the United States of America does not contain the words "separation of church and state," the Bible does not contain the words "spare the rod, spoil the child ." That phrase comes from "Hudibras," a seventeenth-century satirical poem by Englishman Samuel Butler. Note, the poem in question was a *satire.* Butler was not promoting physical punishment and—this is going to surprise a good number of Christian folks—*neither does the Bible!*

The confusion arises because of faulty exegesis of the word *rod.* In the Bible, *rod* is used in two different ways, with two different meanings. When it appears as "a rod" (preceded by the indefinite article) the reference is to an object—a shepherd's staff, a king's scepter, a measuring stick, and yes, a cane used to administer physical punishment. However, when it appears as "the rod" (preceded by the definite article), the reference is to God's authority, as in Isaiah 11:4, where God will judge the poor and "strike the earth with the rod of his mouth." No serious student of Scripture would assert, based on that verse, that a narrow, cylindrical object protrudes from God's mouth. "The rod of His mouth" is a metaphor for God's sovereignty in all matters, the unequivocal authority of His Word.

Remember, parents are to act "in God's image." They are to represent Him to their children. They are to reflect, as well as humanly possible, God's love, and they are to discipline with an authority that properly "mirrors" His. When Proverbs refers to "*the* rod of discipline," the reference is not to corporeal punishment *per se*. In these passages, God is instructing parents to discipline in a godly (composed, authoritative, just) manner—to not let emotion drive the discipline of their children. On some occasions, a spanking is a legitimate expression of the rod of discipline, but God is not enjoining parents to spank every time their children misbehave. Nor is He instructing parents, when they spank, to do so with "rods" of various sorts—belts, paddles, canes, switches, wooden spoons, and the like.

That would make no biblical sense. In Exodus, for example, God decrees that "When a man strikes his slave, male or female, with *a* rod and the slave dies under his hand, he shall be avenged" (21:20, emphasis added). Clearly, striking an adult slave with a sturdy staff may result in the slave's death. In Proverbs 23:13, however, God is unequivocal when it comes to applying *the* rod of discipline: "Do not withhold discipline from a child; if you punish them with *the* rod, they will not die" (NIV, emphasis added). If *a* rod (Exod.) can kill an adult but God promises that application of *the* rod (Prov.) will not kill a child, then these are two entirely different rods. The difference is defined by the preceding articles. Exodus refers to a durable stick, while *the* rod of Proverbs is a metaphor for God's supreme authority.

So, when Proverbs 22:15 says that "the rod of discipline" will drive the foolishness from a child's heart, God is not prescribing a spanking every time a child behaves foolishly. Let's face it, folks, with some children that would require more spankings than a person with a properly functioning conscience could bring himself to administer. Besides, if God is prescribing spankings, and spankings only, for misbehavior, then how is it that some people who were never spanked as children were nonetheless properly behaved kids and grew up to be God-fearing adults? Because God is not prescribing spankings, that's how! His disciplinary instructions to parents define an attitude and a process, not a methodology.

Some folks might well point out that several translations of Proverbs 23:13 (above) use the indefinite article, rendering the phrase in question as "if you strike him with *a rod*, he will not die" (ESV, emphasis added). There may be dispute over whether "the" or "a" is the more appropriate article in some cases, but the glaring discrepancy between *a rod* of Exodus and either *the rod* or *a rod* of Proverbs 23 remains—one can kill while the other will not. In either case, we are left without a blanket prescription for spanking.

So, when I am asked, "Do you believe in spanking, John?" I answer, "No, I don't *believe* in them, but I do think a spanking is the best disciplinary option at certain times and in certain situations, with certain kids."

Parents who spank need to be mindful of four considerations:

1. At some point, spankings become counterproductive. The more spankings a child receives, the less impact any given spanking will have (pun intended). For spankings to be effective, they should be reserved for highly rebellious behavior.
2. Parents have told me that spanking their children for misbehavior made matters worse. Would God, knowing that physical punishment backfires with some kids, make such a blanket recommendation? I don't think so. Besides, God isn't a "methods Guy" when it comes to discipline, much less a one-note methods Guy. He describes an approach, not a set of methods, and the centerpiece of His approach is proper instruction. Yes, God's approach includes consequences, but there is no scriptural support for the idea that He is stuck on one consequence only. If spankings backfire with a certain child,

the solution is not to spank more and harder; it is to use other consequences.

3. Spankings do not require a wooden spoon or belt to qualify as a legitimate form of "the rod of discipline." They can and should be done with the hand. The distinct advantage of using one's hand is that it will experience about as much pain as does the child's rear end; thus, the parent will know when he has inflicted enough justice upon the child and that further swats would be unnecessary.

4. The leading researcher into spanking—research psychologist Robert Larzelere—has found that its usefulness begins to wane around age six, at which time he recommends alternative consequences of the sort described in *The Well-Behaved Child: Discipline That Really Works!* by yours truly (Thomas Nelson, 2011).

And now that we have gotten to the *bottom* of that, we shall *switch* to another topic, hopefully one that will prove equally *handy*.

FOR PERSONAL PONDERING AND GROUP DISCUSSION

1. Does it surprise you to learn that "the rod of discipline" is not necessarily a spanking? If you are willing to accept the interpretation put forth in this chapter, how will that affect your approach to discipline?

2. If you have been a "spanker," are you often spanking for repetitions the same offense? If so, has it occurred to you that the spankings obviously are not working? What other consequences might work as well or better?

3. Look up other scripture that employ the word *rod*. Make two lists, one of scripture that read "the rod" and one of scripture that read "a rod." That should clarify that "the rod" is a metaphor for God's authority.

14
ALPHA SPEECH

But let your "Yes" be "Yes," and your "No," "No." For whatever is more than these is from the evil one.

—*Matthew 5:37 (NKJV)*

During the so-called Sermon on the Mount, Jesus tells his disciples, whom He is preparing to assume His ministry when He departs, to swear no oaths, but speak in plain, emphatic, unequivocal language. Language of that sort is what I call leadership or alpha speech. A person who rightly occupies a position of leadership understands that effective leadership is largely a matter of presentation. Proper leadership is constituted of a certain *attitude,* the primary characteristic of which is the ability to communicate expectations clearly and compel people to do their best.

All the above applies to the raising of a child. Parenting is leadership; therefore, the effective discipline of a child is largely a matter of presentation. Most parents, unfortunately, think effective discipline is largely a matter of manipulating consequences properly. That is why, after parents describe to me a discipline problem with which they are struggling, they nearly always ask, "*What* should I do?" They're asking for a means of using consequences such that the behavior problem in question goes away. Let me be clear: Consequences are necessary to the proper discipline of a child, but they are not the "be all, end all" of proper discipline. Proper consequences delivered without a proper attitude do not work. The key to effective discipline is a correct presentation, and that presentation is largely a matter of leadership speech. Said differently, effective discipline is largely a matter of how parents communicate their expectations and instructions to their children, and in that regard, their speech is key.

Letting your yes be simply yes and your no be simply no means making yourself perfectly clear. Say what you mean, and mean what you say. Yelling at a child is not leadership speech, nor is threatening a child with horrible consequences. Yelling and threatening only communicate that the child has gotten the better of the parent. Consequently, the parent is suddenly down at the child's level. So, the child yells back, and the snowball begins rolling downhill.

On the other side of the coin, cajoling, persuading, and enticing also fail to communicate authority. They communicate to a child that the parent is unsure of himself, uncomfortable with being an authority figure. Once again, the parent is down at the child's level. So, the child ignores the parent, begins to argue, procrastinates, or blatantly refuses to follow orders. After more back and forth, the parent cracks, yells, and the same snowball begins rolling downhill.

A few examples of the difference between leadership speed and "sweet-talk":

Leadership Speech: "It's time for you to stop whatever it is you're doing and begin getting ready for bed."

Sweet-Talk: "Honey, do you think you can stop what you're doing and get ready for bed? Will you do that for Mommy, okay?"

Leadership Speech: "I need you to pick up these toys and move them somewhere else."

Sweet-Talk: "Princess, you could help Mommy by picking up these toys and moving them somewhere else, okay? Pastor is on his way over, and I'd like to serve him coffee in here."

Leadership Speech: "No."

Sweet-Talk: "Honey, I don't know about that. I mean, I know Billy's parents let him do that, but your dad and I, well, we just feel you're not old enough yet. But I'll tell you what! Maybe we can find some responsibility, like a chore, that you can do to earn that privilege! What do you say?"

Those three examples of the difference between authoritative speech and sweet-talk should suffice. One is concise, the other wordy. One is unequivocal, the other wobbly. One comes straight to the point; the other dances around the issue. One is simply "Do this," the other is "I'd really like you to do this because ...." One is an instruction, the other a request.

Disc jockeys take requests. Children, not so much.

FOR PERSONAL PONDERING AND GROUP DISCUSSION

1. What sort of speech—leadership or sweet-talk—is more characteristic of how you give instructions to your child? If you lean toward the latter, what influences are at play?

2. Leadership speech can be learned. In that regard, the appropriate adage is "practice makes perfect." Are you willing to begin practicing leadership speech? If so, the way to do it is to pause before you give your child an instruction and compose, in your head, an instruction that communicates your authority effectively. Then, stand and deliver!

3. Using leadership speech, how would you tell your child to get dressed? How would you tell him to hold your hand while you're crossing the street together? How would you tell him he is not allowed to ride his bike past the stop sign at the end of the street? Remember, practice makes perfect! Well, not perfect maybe, but much better for sure.

15
A MUTUALITY OF EXASPERATION

Fathers, do not exasperate your children; instead, bring them up in the training and instruction of the LORD.

—Ephesians 6:4 (NIV)

Fathers, do not provoke your children to anger, but bring them up in the training and instruction of the LORD.

—Ephesians 6:4 (NASB)

A single mother sought my advice concerning her fourteen-year-old son: "No matter what consequences I use when he misbehaves, like when he talks back," she said, "he goes bonkers, like, completely out of control. He yells at me, storms off to his room, slams the door, and begins screaming like he's being tortured with a cattle prod. It sometimes takes him a full day to calm down. Obviously, my discipline is provoking him to anger. I must be doing something wrong."

Because her discipline (i.e., punitive consequences) upset her teenage son, sometimes to the point of rage, this mother was convinced she was not disciplining him properly. She cited Ephesians 6:4 as the basis for her conclusion.

"It says my discipline shouldn't upset him, right?" she asked.

No, that's not right. Ephesians 6:4 is surely on the short list of most misunderstood Scripture. Contrary to what many Christians think (and even some pastors preach), Paul is not telling parents that their discipline should never upset their children. That would contradict Hebrews 12:11 (chapter 24), which says that effective discipline should be discomforting to the recipient.

As should be obvious to anyone with children, they do not relish being disciplined. They generally resent it, in fact. As a mature thirteen-year-old boy told me, "I usually get upset when my parents discipline me. I think whatever they've done is unfair, but when I calm down and think about it, I almost always agree they did the right thing." Note that the lad's typical first reaction to being disciplined is defensive and emotional—*foolish*—but when he regains his ability to think straight, he puts his parents' actions into proper perspective.

The single mom in the above anecdote was intimidated by her son's very exaggerated reaction to being punished. Based on her misinterpretation of Ephesians 6:4, she believed that his reaction meant her discipline was inappropriate. She responded by trying to discipline him without offending his sensitivities. Consequently, instead of driving foolishness out of his heart, she was enabling it. Furthermore, her enabling had caused the parent–child relationship to turn upside-down. Power in the relationship had shifted to the boy, and he was exercising that power to push his mother around, figuratively speaking. A vicious cycle had developed: The more mom tried to discipline without upsetting her live-in tyrant, the more of a tyrant he became, causing her even more uncertainty, and around and around they went.

The common misinterpretation of Ephesians 6:4 comes about because people only pay attention to the first half of the verse: "Fathers, do not exasperate your children [or, provoke your children to anger]." But God does not speak in half-verses. As is the case with any scripture, this one cannot be properly understood unless it is read in its entirety, paying close attention to every word. Approached in that fashion, it becomes obvious that the verse in question turns on the word *instead:* "Fathers, do not exasperate your children; *instead,* bring them up in the training and instruction of the LORD [emphasis added]."

When the entire verse is considered, it becomes a warning. Paul is telling parents that if they do not raise their children "in the training and instruction of the LORD," they are virtually guaranteed to "exasperate" them or "provoke them to anger." Synonyms of *provoke* include goad, incite, bait, needle, irritate, and inflame—words that refer to *deliberate,* even sadistic, attempts to upset someone. Ephesians 6:4, therefore, establishes a prohibition against parental discipline that serves no constructive purpose; especially parental discipline that is vengeful or retaliatory instead of instructive. Paul is referring to an erratic, emotion-driven parenting style—the antithesis of bringing up a child in the "training and instruction of the LORD." Paul employs that phrase to refer to parent behavior that conforms to the standard established by God and put an exclamation point on the fact that in raising children, parents are responsible for representing God properly.

Discipline consists of constructive teaching and correction. It is the process by which parents, acting as God's representatives, influence their children toward becoming, first, *their* disciples, and later, disciples of the Lord Jesus. In other words, at some point in the process of raising a child, usually around ages twelve or thirteen, parents should be able to hand the "baton" of a child's discipleship to Christ. Effective parental discipline—establishing and enforcing rules, responsibilities, and boundaries—eventually results in positive change to a child's head and heart. The child thinks more clearly, with an ever-better understanding of what is true, right, and good, and is more capable of self-restraint. As that process moves forward, his ability to think straight and exercise self-control steadily improves. As the Spirit transforms him into a disciple of Christ, the child becomes liberated, one step at a time, from his slavery to sin.

When parents bring up their children according to sources other than God's Word—sources that reflect man's own thinking (see Colossians 2:8, chapter 3)—they invariably zig, zag, weave, wobble, and backtrack about the parenting playing field in constant search of faddish "answers." Untethered to God's Word, an individual becomes vulnerable to progressive ideas, and his thinking on any given subject becomes prone to change without notice (aka confusion). Likewise, as parents read parenting book after parenting book, they try one method and approach after another, but the parenting books they are reading (the exceptions are rare, even in the Christian parenting genre) are more in line with man's whims than with God's perfect plan for the raising of children. Because they are following parenting fads and advice that largely ignore or even deny the sin nature of children, their parenting behavior is marked by inconstancy, indecision, and volatility. Under the circumstances, their children can neither understand their parents' purpose nor predict how they are going to react from one situation to the next. The sort of parent being described gives a child a certain permission one day and withholds it the next; is calm and composed one day but flies off the handle the next; is understanding and accommodating one day but rigidly intolerant the next. That unpredictability, that flipping and flopping from situation to situation, will most definitely *exasperate* a child; and to paraphrase Forrest Gump, exasperation is as exasperation does. An exasperated child is the counterpart of parents who are equally exasperated. Because they have no reliable roadmap, they are in a near-perpetual state of parenting muddle.

"I'm a yeller," says a parent. "It's like I'm hard-wired to blow up at my kids."

That is simply not true. Periodic loss of composure is not built into someone's DNA, like one's eye color. Yelling at one's kids is the consequence of exasperation, and exasperation is the inevitable consequence of not parenting according to God's instructions. Blending Proverbs 3:6 (chapter 38) and Ephesians 6:4 results in a parenting principle that reads:

The parenting path of someone who raises his kids in keeping with his own and other people's understandings—as opposed to raising them in "the training and instruction of the LORD"— will surely not be straight, and that lack of "straightness" will be exasperating to both him and his children.

To remind the reader, Christian parents complain of the same child-rearing problems as do secular parents. In today's topsy-turvy world, Christian and secular parents are equally exasperated. That can mean only one thing: *Most Christian parents are raising their children according to the very same understandings adhered to by most secular parents.* If that is true, and I believe it is, then Christian parents are failing to distinguish themselves from the world when it comes to their child-rearing priorities and practices. That, in fact, may be the most begging problem of all in the Christian community.

What does provocative or exasperating discipline look like? A parent is being *provocative* when his response to misbehavior is merely *retaliatory* in nature. Almost without exception, the parent in question *personalizes* the child's misconduct, as if it is a personal affront, and becomes angry, even out of control. The parent's response to the child's misdeed is knee-jerk, vengeful, and unjust—an "I'll show you!" comeback. The parent allows emotion to drive his disciplinary behavior. For that reason, his response to his child's sin is itself childish and sinful and cannot help but provoke a like reaction—highly emotional, that is—from the child. At that flashpoint, parent and child begin spiraling downward into a state of mutual irrationality. Nothing constructive is accomplished, and the emotional disciplinary drama is destined to be repeated.

Biblical correction, on the other hand, is not provocative. Discipline— even significant punishment—is delivered in a calm, thoughtful, albeit compelling and memorable manner. When a child misbehaves, the operative question is "How, in this situation, do I best teach my child the need to control his sin nature?" To let the heat of the moment subside, carefully consider one's disciplinary options, and make a decision based on the answer to that question is not going to result in discipline that is provocative, *even though it may be temporarily upsetting to the child.* I cannot stress enough that a child's reaction to being disciplined does not tell the story of its appropriateness or lack thereof.

Another way of looking at this issue is to point out that punishment and justice are not necessarily the same thing. Chapter 6 dealt with a parent's responsibility to act as God's representative, His proxy, in the raising of children. When God disciplines, His discipline is always perfectly just. He may be terrifying when He disciplines—sending poisonous snakes to kill rebellious Israelites, for example (Num. 21:6)—but His discipline is always, without exception, perfectly righteous and perfectly just. Unlike God, however, parents are flawed human beings. Therefore, when parents discipline, especially when they mete out punishment, they are in danger of behaving in ways that do not approximate God's justice; in ways, that is, that are impulsive, retaliatory, and not truly corrective. That sort of discipline is *provocative*. It does not instruct. It only exasperates.

Mind you, under no circumstances should corrective discipline feel, to the recipient, neutral. Corrective discipline should "sting." It should excite the recipient's emotions, but the intention is to cause not anger (although that may be, as in the above example, the child's initial response), but contrition, repentance, and self-correction. To repeat myself, children do not welcome being disciplined. They take no delight in being corrected, much less having to endure punitive consequences. As was the case with Adam and Eve, children can be counted on to try to avoid responsibility for misbehavior (e.g., lying, passing the buck of responsibility, arguing). Even the most proper, godly discipline may precipitate an emotional reaction. Nonetheless, punitive discipline is at times the only just response to a child's misbehavior.

It may be helpful to conceive of discipline as the act of pushing something formidable up a hill, against the force of gravity. Likewise, proper discipline pushes against the "gravity" of a child's sin nature. As discipline from parents, teachers, and other adults moves the child's sin nature "uphill," it is gradually displaced and replaced—never completely, mind you, but to significant degree—by a love of God and a prosocial disposition (love of neighbor). The process is laborious, for sure. The discipline of a child sometimes involves taking two steps forward and then one step back. Ever so slowly, with great perseverance on the part of his or her parents, the child puts childish things behind him (1 Cor. 13:11) and begins growing into authentic adulthood.

That uphill process requires diligence, perseverance, patience, resolve, a willingness to suffer setback, and unconditional love. As the adage says, "No pain, no gain." That uphill struggle is often painful for both parent and child. But parents have a promise from God: if they persevere, a harvest of righteousness and peace is to be had for all concerned (Heb. 12:11, chapter 24). Proper discipline is a blessing to a child, but the child is not likely to think of it as such until the battle is won.

FOR PERSONAL PONDERING AND GROUP DISCUSSION

1. Do you recognize yourself in the description of a parent whose discipline is driven by emotion? If so, what specific things can you begin doing to bring your child-rearing into better alignment with God's instruction?

2. In practical, day-to-day terms, what does it look like to raise a child according to the "training and instruction of the LORD"? Think of five concrete characteristics of godly child-rearing that set it distinctly apart from the sort of child-rearing you see going on around you.

3. How can parents armor themselves against peer-group pressure to raise children in line with worldly (unbiblical) standards that are self-defeating but "popular"?

16

THE HOLY PURPOSE
OF TRADITION

Honor your father and your mother so that you may live long in
the land the Lord your God is giving you.
　　　　　　　—Exodus 20:12 (also see Deut. 5:16; Eph. 6:2)

After a talk I gave to a church audience in California, a fellow introduced himself as a high school history teacher and shared his enthusiasm
for teaching his students about the 1960s.

"I point out that the rebelliousness of the 1960s was a reaction to the
conformity of the 1950s," he said.

He was moved by my description of the paradigm shift America
underwent in the 1960s and early 1970s, during which we uprooted
ourselves from nearly all that represented tradition, the old ways, and
became a full-fledged postmodern, progressive culture. Among other
things, that realignment transformed mere child-rearing into what has
since been called *parenting.* Pertinent to this anecdote is the fact that the
fellow in question was in his mid-thirties at the time of our encounter,
or so I surmised from his appearance and demeanor. Assuming I am
correct, he was born around 1980. He can be forgiven, therefore, for not
knowing what he was talking about. His take on the 1960s, undoubtedly

informed by what he had been taught by liberal history professors, was way off the mark.

Not one to mince words, I said, "The commonly held notion that the 1950s was a time of witless mass conformity is a myth. You're mistaking near-universal agreement on fundamental issues and values with mindless group-think."

In the 1960s, the toxic floodwaters of relativism (ever-shifting secular definitions of good *versus* evil and truth *versus* falsehood), which had been slowly rising for quite some time, breached the levees and began to destroy the *United* in United States of America. Relativists propose, in brief, that absolute truth is a fiction; that moral standards are matters of place (culture) and time (historical era). Because those standards are not fixed, the individual is free to choose, based on current fashions and personal taste, where to draw the line between right and wrong. Relativists also believe that the more recent the standard, the more enlightened it is. Thus, post-1960s attitudes toward abortion, homosexuality, pedophilia, and divorce are supposedly more enlightened than standards established thousands of years ago. That progressive ball got rolling when the serpent succeeded at convincing Eve that by eating of the forbidden tree, she could define good and evil for herself, independent of God's eternal standards, and become "like God" in wisdom (Gen. 3:5).

One of the pseudo-intellectual memes that came out of the 1960s is the appealing notion that the key to universal peace and brotherly love is respect for and tolerance of any point of view, no matter how different it is from the biblical or historical standard. As a popular platitude of the day put it, "I'm okay, you're okay." That is an expression of relativism in pure form. It is a very alluring and seductive form of false knowledge and has been since the garden. The problem is that false understandings always lead to wrong thinking and counterproductive (sinful) behavior.

No, the 1950s was not a time of mass conformity. That canard is essential to maintaining romantic delusions about the decade that followed—the 1960s. The delusions in question are necessary to persuade the gullible that today's cultural revisionists are only trying to fulfill the (demonic) *quest for social perfection* that began in that very deconstructive decade. The truth about the 1950s is that most people agreed about fundamental things like values and morality, and where there was disagreement, it was generally minor. A pertinent FACT:

Fundamental agreement concerning foundational principles sustains culture and as such ensures that people will enjoy living "long in the land the Lord [has given them]."

One of the most fundamental, if not *the single most fundamental* of social agreements pertains to how the family should be structured and children should be raised. Those standards, founded on biblical principle, were brought to America by the colonists and prevailed until the modern era. In the 1950s and before, nearly everyone in the United States of America raised children in the same fashion. There was, for example, universal agreement that the family should be adult-centric. So, in the 1950s home, parents ruled the roost. Moreover, the 1950s mother and father were husband and wife first and parents second. Children had obligations to their families. They were expected to be respectful and responsible in both the community and the home. In addition, they had chores which they were expected to do on time, properly, without being reminded, and for which they were not paid. They did their own homework, studied independently for tests, and were generally held to high academic standards. They organized their own games, settled their own quarrels, bandaged their own cuts, and were never, ever in the right when a responsible adult said otherwise.

My parents and my friends' parents were interchangeable. They all set the bar at the same height. They agreed on what was right *versus* what was wrong, and when a child did something wrong, they all sent the same unequivocal message: "Don't do it again, lest you force me to do something even worse than what I did this time."

God's Fifth Commandment means more than treating one's parents with respect; it also means continuing their traditions and adhering to the principles and values that shaped and defined their lives. Those traditions and principles include those that pertain to child-rearing—again, a foundational human activity. Many young parents, upon hearing that traditionalist message, express skepticism. "But times have changed!" they exclaim, implying that as the world changes, everything, including how children are raised, should change along with it. But times have always changed. Throughout the history of Western Civilization (which began with Abraham and Sarah), every generation has brought innovation into culture. There is, however, no evidence that until the psychological parenting revolution of the late 1960s and early 1970s, the understandings that informed child-rearing in Western Civilization ever changed. Every new generation honored its ancestors—its "fathers and mothers"—by raising children according to traditional understandings. Thus, the parenting baton was handed down from one generation to the next. As times changed, the fundamentals of child-rearing remained constant. Each generation dealt with a certain number of novel child-rearing considerations, but they dealt with them in the same way their foremothers and forefathers dealt with equally novel child-rearing considerations.

My generation, when it came time to take the parenting baton from our parents—the so-called Greatest Generation—rejected it. We let it fall into the dirt. We thought we had better ideas of how to properly raise kids, by which we meant ideas that stood in complete opposition to our parents' ideas, which they had received from their parents who had received them from their parents and so on. The new ideas were cut from whole cloth by people representing the mental health professions. Upon consuming the progressive ideas in question, we Boomers—not all of us, of course, but enough of us to make a huge difference—became determined to change the world. Utopia was at hand, and we were intoxicated by the soothing hiss of its promise.

When the intergenerational transmission of fundamental traditions and principles is disrupted, a culture's unity begins to unravel, and its strength begins to wane. Thus, we are, as I write, the Disrupted, Disjointed, Destabilized, and Dispirited States of America. It's a sorry state of affairs, one that is not going to be solved by more bipartisanship in the chambers of government or more tax dollars being spent on schools or social programs. Man, leaning on his own understandings (Prov. 3:5, chapter 38), created the problem. Only by trusting completely in God's Word will man be able to solve it.

The conservative-traditionalist believes there is nothing new under the sun (Eccles. 1:9, chapter 17). The progressive believes new ideas are better than old ideas. My parents believed there was nothing about raising me they could not learn from the example of their parents. On the other hand, my wife and I, because we fell under the sway of new ideas, believed that by following advice dispensed by the New Pied Pipers of postmodern psychological parenting, we would raise our kids much, much better than we had been raised. Some lessons can only be learned the hard way (see the Epilogue).

This book celebrates the old ways. It is a song of praise to the principles that guided American child-rearing before "experts" took the wheel, drove us into a ditch, and then convinced us that the ditch was where we should have been all along. Consider that since American parents began taking their marching orders from psychologists and other mental health professionals, the mental health of American children has taken, and is still taking, a nosedive. Today's child is ten times more likely than was a child raised in the 1950s to experience a serious emotional problem by age sixteen. Millions of children are taking psychiatric drugs to help them control distractibility, depression, and anxiety. The numbers tell the real story of psychology's impact on child-rearing, and the story is not good in any respect.

America is in desperate need of a parenting retro-revolution, a restoration of traditional, biblical child-rearing principles. This book is a contribution to that effort. If the effort succeeds, it will do so not because of experts. It will succeed because people have had enough. Have you?

FOR PERSONAL PONDERING AND GROUP DISCUSSION

1. How different is your approach to parenting from your parents' approach? How about your grandparents' approach (if you have knowledge of it)? Are you faring better? Are your kids as well-behaved, respectful, and responsible as you were?

2. In the way you are raising your children, have you bought into the progressive notion that the newer the idea the better? What difficulties might you not be having had you "honored your father and mother" when it came to child-rearing?

3. What retro-steps will bring your parenting into closer alignment with tradition and God's plan? What do you think the benefits of making such a U-turn would be to you personally, your marriage, and your kids?

17
GRANDMA WAS RIGHT AFTER ALL!

That which has been *is* what will be,
That which *is* done is what will be done,
And *there is* nothing new under the sun.

—*Ecclesiastes 1:9 (NKJV)*

A grandmother sadly relates that upon trying to give her adult daughter advice concerning the behavior of her three-year-old grandchild, the daughter snapped, "You don't know him well enough to be giving me advice!" That is the quintessential post-1960s parent talking. Many of today's parents are enamored of the notion that a child's upbringing needs to be informed primarily by personality quirks or some exceptionality— by, in other words, attributes that make him *unique*. Granted, every child brings a one-of-a-kind personality into the world with him. But whereas every child's outward social presentation is distinctive, every child's fundamental *nature* is a constant. Another way of saying the same thing: expression changes; essence does not. The attributes that define *human* have not changed since Adam and Eve. Furthermore, that sameness is far more significant—more innate, profound, predictive, and essential to a proper understanding of *any* child—than some distinct aspect of personality, IQ, or a bogus diagnosis obtained from a mental health professional.

When the Word of God proclaims that "there is nothing new under the sun," it is obviously not referring to technologies because the history of mankind is largely the history of innovation. Rather, the writer of Ecclesiastes (King David's son, Solomon, presumably) is referring to right ideas, principles, understandings, and concepts, all of which inform a right way of living. "Nothing new under the sun" refers to the proper way of regarding and approaching the demands of life. This oft-quoted scripture, when applied specifically to child-rearing, can be paraphrased:

Despite what you've heard and perhaps been led to believe by various progressive parenting pundits, there is nothing new under the sun when it comes to properly raising a child.

Correct understandings of right and wrong, good and evil, truth and falsehood do not change from generation to generation. In the Bible, God has set forth a code by which He wants us, His proxies, to raise His children. The principles constituting that code are timeless, unchanging, forever. They are not subject to periodic update. They are as right today as they ever have been. There is but one proper way, therefore, to raise one of God's children.

The contemporary parent comes by her tunnel vision honestly, to be sure. The parenting section of a bookstore is replete with titles promoting the idea that raising a child properly requires first knowing what "kind" of child one is dealing with. Has the child been diagnosed with ADHD or some other phony "disorder"? Is he learning disabled? Adopted? A twin? A middle? An oldest? An only? On and on the categories go, with more to come next week. The implication is that a child should be raised according to a set of guidelines unique to the subset of *children* to which he rightly belongs. The fact is, one does not need to know Billy/Billie in all of his/her supposedly distinctive facets to know that there is but *one* proper way to raise Billy/Billie. The way in question is not found in the parenting section of a bookstore, but in the religious section, under Bibles. Beware, however, because the Bible's parenting "way" is very old-fashioned stuff, and among today's young-adult generation, there are relatively few who want to be found embracing that which is old in any respect.

And so, when a grandmother tries to relay some old-fashioned parenting advice to her daughter, the daughter denies that Grandma—who has lived twice as many years and raised twice as many children—knows of what she speaks. In so doing, this very progressively-minded daughter dishonors her mother's wisdom and experience. Grandma does not understand her daughter's reaction. When she was a new parent, she *valued* her mother's advice. It did not matter that her mother lived halfway across the country and only saw her grandchildren once a year for a week or so. Her mother understood children. She had raised seven, after all. Her mother knew that every child is born with an individual personality, but that a child's innate inclination toward sin (self-serving antisocial behavior) must be of primary consideration when it comes to his upbringing. Here are the key understandings:

a. Every child is strong-willed and rebellious, only some are more overt, less subtle about it than others.
b. In any given choice situation, a child is more inclined to do what reflects love of self than what reflects love of others.
c. Properly socializing and preparing the heart of the strong-willed, self-centered child requires a combination of powerful love and equally powerful discipline.

That's it! End of story. Not complicated at all. What, pray tell, was so mysterious about the above grandchild's behavior that Grandma needed to better know him to give her daughter good advice? In a nutshell, his mother told him not to get down from the table with a piece of pizza in his hand. He did anyway. The family dog promptly snatched his pizza and ate it. He cried. Mom gave him another piece of pizza. Grandma tried to point out that he disobeyed and was effectively being rewarded for doing so. Uh-oh. If Mom punishes Grandma consistently enough when she tries to give advice, Grandma will stop "misbehaving." The problem is that Mom is punishing the wrong person. Therefore, the wrong person will stop misbehaving.

FOR PERSONAL PONDERING AND GROUP DISCUSSION

1. To what extent and in what specific ways have you allowed yourself to become convinced there is something new under the sun concerning children and proper child-rearing? What might your parenting look like today if you had believed, all along, in traditional understandings and approaches?

2. When it comes to how you are raising your kids, have you been thinking in terms of categories they fit into such as "adopted," "gifted," or perhaps some pseudo-scientific diagnosis like ADHD? Have you allowed an idiosyncratic attribute to lead you down one child-rearing rabbit hole after another in search of an approach that matches the attribute in question? If so, what would your child-rearing look like if you had simply raised your child with clear consideration of his or her sin nature?

3. Are you completely open to child-rearing advice from your elders, or do you possess a tendency to become defensive or blasé when an older person tries to give you some words of wisdom? Can you think of advice from an elder that you initially rejected, only to discover later that the elder was spot on?

18
FLY HIGH, FALL HARD

Whoever exalts himself will be humbled, and whoever humbles himself will be exalted.

—*Matthew 23:12*

On January 1, 1970, California family counselor Dorothy Briggs's *Your Child's Self-Esteem* (Doubleday) appeared on bookshelves across America. The publication date was auspicious, as if it heralded the end of the old, benighted way of raising children and the beginning of a new way that promised better parents, better children, and a better world. The naked baby on the cover, beaming joyfully, his privates exposed to the world, said it all. *Your Child's Self-Esteem* became a lasting best-seller in the new "parenting" field. Briggs was the protégé of California psychologist Thomas Gordon, author of *Parent Effectiveness Training,* another huge best-seller, also published in 1970. As of 2020, *Parent Effectiveness Training* had been published in thirty-three languages and sold five million copies. It is safe to say that Briggs and Gordon were the prime architects of postmodern psychological parenting, the centerpiece of which is the demonic notion that a high level of regard for oneself (aka self-esteem) is essential to good mental health.

The entire mental health professional community rallied around Briggs's and Gordon's *nouveau* ideas. With the help of an adoring media,

they went quickly viral. Parents began taking up the cause of instilling self-esteem in children. Accomplishing that, claimed Briggs and
Gordon, required that families become democratic and child-centered.
Children needed boatloads of positive attention and praiseful reinforcement. Children had to be treated as their parents' equals. They had
to be included, from toddlerhood, in family decision-making. Parents
were obligated to explain themselves to their children. They were to
never, ever "pull rank," much less "lay down the law." Any difference of
opinion between a parent and a child was to be negotiated until a win-
win outcome was achieved. Punishment was *verboten,* of course. When
a child misbehaved, the parents were to explain why what he had done
was, um, wrong—*No! Never say that a child did something wrong! That
word causes a child to feel worthless and stinky! Say something like, "I feel
uncomfortable when you do that." Own the problem*! Okay, so parents were
to explain how uncomfortable or sad they felt about the values-neutral
things their children did and propose better alternatives. There was to
be no punishment, ever, about anything because punishment caused
children to feel worthless and stinky.

I'm kidding, right? No. Nor am I exaggerating one whit. The family
was to become a microcosm of a utopian society from which badness
had been banished, everyone was equal, no one represented authority,
and truth in any given situation was up for discussion. Those conditions, when they exist in a culture, define socialism in its pure form.
The purveyors of this new family philosophy, I propose, were laying
the groundwork for transforming America into a socialist state, and
wittingly so.

The reality is that no philosophy can alter the unalterable fact that
parents and children are not equals. Children need adults who are
willing to guarantee their safety and well-being. Until children are old
enough to take full responsibility for themselves, they need to obey
those adults. Children do not know what the best course of action is
in any given situation. Negotiating to win-win with a child is impossible because children don't understand win-win. They want what they
want, and they believe the ends justify the means. Children believe in
win-lose. So, to create the impression that win-win had been achieved

in one of these socialistic parent-child negotiations, the parents had to lose and act like everybody had won. Billy, age sixteen, has gotten three speeding tickets in the last three weeks. His parents want to yank his driving privileges. He protests with great drama. His parents back off and negotiate an agreement with Billy that allows him to continue driving if he promises to be more careful. So, Billy agrees to drive more carefully. Win-win? LOL!

To build Billy's self-esteem, his parents and teachers (this ho-hah quickly infiltrated America's schools) had to pretend that everything he did and said was hunky-dory. One of the more popular parenting adages of the 1970s was "Catch 'em being good!" According to people with capital letters after their names, praising a child for every "good" thing he did—as in, "Billy, I really appreciate it when you don't call me vile names during a difference of opinion"—would result, over time, in more and more good and less and less bad. Oh! Sorry. I almost forgot. Nothing Billy does is *bad* in the first place. His behavior infuriates his parents sometimes, yes, but that's their problem, and they have to own it.

Laugh if you will, but again, I'm not kidding.

Mind you, not one iota of this *nouveau* philosophy had been subjected to the rigors of the scientific method. People like Briggs and Gordon pulled this progressive stuff out of thin air. They were selling a pig in a poke; nonetheless, people lined up to buy it.

Beginning in the 1980s, several social scientists put Briggs's and Gordon's theories, especially self-esteem theory, to the test. They discovered that most people with high levels of self-esteem were manipulative and controlling, even sociopathic. One researcher discovered that hardcore criminals had higher levels of self-esteem than people in any other population group. Interestingly, studies also found that high levels of self-esteem were associated with periodic episodes of clinical depression. It seems the folks in question cannot handle the ups and downs of the real world very well at all. Women in relationships with men who fit the high self-esteem profile are in grave danger of being abused because the men in question have never grown up—like "terrible" two-year-olds, they lash out at people who don't give them their way. By the way, it is significant to note that one of the researchers in question said that since the 1960s, parents had done a great job of instilling self-esteem into America's kids. He was being sardonic.

Since the early 1970s, when Brigg's and Gordon's ideas went viral, the mental health of children and teens has spiraled downward. The child-centered family has contributed significantly to an exponential increase in the rate of divorce, and a good percentage of kids raised in these upside-down, inside-out families are now adults who shun marriage and child-rearing. Lest one think that Briggs's and Gordon's nutty and destructive philosophies have run their course, consider that in January of 2017, forty-seven years after the publications of *Your Child's Self-Esteem* and *Parent Effectiveness Training,* the influential *Wall Street Journal* featured an article by California parent educator Jennifer Lehr, author of *PARENTSPEAK: What's Wrong with How We Talk to Our Children—and What to Say Instead* (Workman, 2017). On her website, Lehr cites the "democratic decision-making principals" (sic), of Thomas Gordon as one of her primary inspirations.

The serpent is a tenacious fellow, indeed.

FOR PERSONAL PONDERING AND GROUP DISCUSSION

1. Has your parenting approach been influenced, however unwittingly, by Brigg's and Gordon's progressive philosophy? If so, how?

2. Which of Briggs's and Gordon's ideas has caused you, your children, and your family the greatest difficulty? The democratic family? The supposed need for you to explain yourself to your children? The supposed need to lavish praise on your kids at every possible opportunity?

3. What is the biblical opposite of self-esteem? Why is that biblical opposite essential to good mental health and a proper biblical worldview?

19
THE BLESSINGS OF FEAR

The fear of the Lord is the beginning of wisdom, and knowledge
of the Holy One is insight.

—Proverbs 9:10

And he said to man, "Behold, the fear of the Lord, that is
wisdom, and to turn away from evil is understanding."

—Job 28:28

To fear the Lord is not to be constantly terrified of Him, albeit terror
may be appropriate at certain times, in the case of certain persons. To
fear the Lord, as in Proverbs 9:10, is to be in awe of His holiness, power,
purity, and sovereignty over everything seen and unseen. His creation
is wisdom itself; therefore, to possess awestruck reverence for all He has
done is to possess insight. The ability to properly discern good and evil—
to seek and embrace what is good and renounce what is evil—begins
with fear of the Lord.

After describing her five-year-old daughter's tantrums, disobedience,
and disrespect—all of which were magnificently horrid—a mother asked
if I could help her figure out the "issues" her daughter was "grappling
with."

"She's not grappling with any issues," I said. "She's simply not afraid of you."

"Oh! Well, I really don't want her to be afraid of me," she replied.

"Then I can't help you," I said to her astonishment. Nonetheless, she later told me that the ensuing conversation with me had been a first step in both her and her daughter's rehabilitations.

Today's parents—not all of them, of course, but probably most—have great difficulty wrapping their heads around the idea that their children *should* fear them—not be terrified of them but nevertheless fearful. The parents in question have been persuaded by psychological propaganda that good parenting is all about having a delightful parent–child *relationship*. Because they prioritize relationship, their ability to effect leadership suffers and their kids have no fear of them. Thus, per the horrid little girl in the above anecdote, these well-meaning parents experience discipline problems of a sort unheard of three generations ago, when children feared adult authority and had far fewer mental health issues.

The "fear" in question is not akin to what a person experiences upon encountering a grizzly bear in the wilderness. The fear of a child toward his or her parents is a biblical fear of the sort one should possess toward God. The Bible tells us that fear of the Lord "leads to life" (Pro. 19:23), is "hatred of evil" (Prov. 8:13), and enables one to "turn away from the snares of death" (Prov. 14:27). God is merciful to those who fear him (Luke 1:50). Fear of the Lord "endures forever" and imputes righteousness (Ps. 19:9). To sum it all up, nothing but good comes of fearing God. Important to note is that the good things that come from fearing God come to those who fear him! No Bible verse says anything along the lines of "God feels pumped when people fear Him" or "God obtains affirmation by causing people to fear Him." Every Bible verse that speaks to the benefits of fearing the Lord describes benefits that come to those who possess proper fear.

Obedience is the best measure of a child's fear of his parents. The more a child fears his parents in the biblical sense—that is, respects their authority, their dominion, in his life—the more obedient the child will be. Is there evidence that fearful obedience on the part of a child is beneficial to the child? Yes, there certainly is! Social science researchers have discovered that a child's sense of well-being—the confidence that he is unconditionally loved and has nothing to worry about (confidence that his parents are "taking care of business")—is directly proportionate to the child's level of obedience. Said another way, the more obedient a child, the more secure the child. Even more succinctly: An obedient child is a happy child! Fear of the Lord is expressed in obedience to Him. The psalmist wrote, "Blessed is the man who fears the Lord, who greatly delights in His commandments!" (Ps. 112:1). The man who obeys the Lord is blessed. And note that the fear in question does not involve anxiety, dread, apprehension, or panic. The man in question "greatly delights" in his own obedience. As with a child, an obedient adult is a happy adult!

Parents are obligated to both God and their children to see to it that their children fear them in the biblical sense. For better or worse, parents are a child's first understanding of a Supreme Being. As God's representatives, parents are obligated to be equally loving and authoritative toward their children, as He is equally loving and authoritative with us. By representing Him as accurately as they are humanly capable, parents endow their children with moral, spiritual, and emotional strength and lead them toward understanding that God is the source of all endurance. No amount of worldly success outweighs those blessings.

At one point, the above mom asked, "How do I get my daughter to fear me?"

"Begin by acting like you know what you are doing," I said. "Act like you do not need her help making decisions and that you don't care what she thinks of any decision you make. Most of all, stop second-guessing yourself and equivocating and enforce your expectations and instructions with firm resolve. In short, you need to learn how to be mean."

"Mean?"

"Yes, mean," I said. "From your daughter's point of view, you will ascend the 'Mean Mommy Throne' when she discovers that you mean what you say without exception."

Blessed is the child with a calmly mean mommy! (And daddy, too, of course.)

FOR PERSONAL PONDERING AND GROUP DISCUSSION

1. In your child-rearing, have you prioritized having delightful relationships with your children over providing them unequivocal leadership? If so, what have the consequences been to both you and your kids? Does parenting stress you out? Do your kids have anxiety issues? Are they disobedient and disrespectful? Do they throw frequent tantrums?

2. Do you need to reshuffle your parenting priorities and put more emphasis on authority and discipline? If so, how, exactly, do you intend to do that?

3. As a parent, are you acting like you know what you are doing or are you acting like you need their help making decisions? Have your children discovered that you are "mean"? If not, what can you begin doing to instill that "fearful" understanding?

20

THE LAST SEAT IN
THE LIFEBOAT

Greater love has no one than this: to lay down one's life for one's friends.

—*John 15:13*

If Ming the Merciless, Emperor of the Universe (I'm dating myself here), captured you and one of your children, and told you that one of you was going to die a gruesome death and that *you* had to decide who died, you or your child, the decision would be a no-brainer, right?

Okay, so here's another no-brainer: If you and one of your children suddenly found yourselves on a sinking ship, and the last lifeboat had but one seat left, would you take it or give it to your child? I told you it was a no-brainer.

In both situations, you would give your life to save your child's. But what if the decision in each of the above scenarios had to be made by your child? What if Ming the Merciless, after describing the most gruesome death in the history of the universe, turned to your child and said, "Okay, kid, you choose." What if the captain of the ship—he's going down with it, remember—after pointing out that only one more person would fit into the last lifeboat, told your child to choose which of you would watch from the lifeboat as the ship disappeared beneath the waves?

In both instances your beloved child would turn to you and say something along the lines of "Sorry, Ma, but well, you understand. It's been nice knowing you." Right? Right!

I'll get back to that, but first, after a presentation during which I had told the audience that children needed their parents to act like superior beings, which was accomplished in large part by properly conveying authority, a fellow approached me and told me he had trouble conceiving of himself as superior to his five-year-old son.

"I think of my son and myself as equals," he said. Dorothy Briggs and Thomas Gordon strike again! How sad, really. With the best of intentions, this fellow is depriving his son of an authentically masculine role model, which is the equivalent to depriving one's child, male or female, of a fundamental understanding of God's loving authority (Eph. 5:25–33). A human role model is someone to whom another person looks up and aspires to become. Neither person in a relationship of equals is going to aspire to become like the other person. If that were the case, they would not be equals.

By the way, this fellow was speaking for many fathers in his generation. I call them "Buddy Dads" because the enlightened modern dad is supposed to be, first and foremost, his child's best buddy. He is not supposed to be a guy who models traditional masculine virtues—emotional control, loyalty, chastity, respect of women, care and protection of women and children—much less a disciplinarian (heaven forbid!). All too often, once the modern husband becomes a father, his priority shifts to relationship with his kids. His free time is often spent coming up with new ways of entertaining them and otherwise demonstrating his commitment to "buddyhood"—which, I cannot overstress, is essentially a relationship of *de facto* equals.

If I had been able to speak at some length with this well-intentioned fellow, I could have easily proven to him that no matter how hard he tried, his quest to be his son's equal was doomed to failure. As the above thought problems irrefutably demonstrate, in the parent–child relationship, only the parent is willing to make the supreme sacrifice.

The child only hopes the parent will make the supreme sacrifice. As such, the parent is clearly the child's moral superior, and morality—not the ability to intimidate—is the defining attribute of authentic superiority. No fantasies of father–child equality will change that fact.

A child can, however, acquire the false impression that he is in fact his parent's equal. That illusion becomes likely when the parent abdicates authority in the attempt to be liked by the child. A person who occupies a leadership position cannot exercise effective authority over someone with whom he wants a buddy–buddy relationship. Invariably, the person who is in the naturally subordinate position ends up resenting it when his buddy-boss pulls rank. Nearly every time I counsel with parents whose kids are shamelessly disobedient and disrespectful, the parents eventually admit to not wanting to upset their kids, ever. Why? Because they want their kids to like them! They give them lots of choices, which leads to argument. They explain their rules and decisions, as if a decision is only binding if the child understands and consents to it. More arguments ensue. They capitulate to tantrums. They apologize to their children on a somewhat regular basis. They negotiate with them, which nearly always results in the child getting most if not all of what he wants. They pay their kids for making their beds in the morning. I hope the reader appreciates the absurdity of parents who buy their children's food, prepare their meals, pay the mortgage and utility bills, pay for their children's clothes and entertainment—all at no cost to the children—but then turn around and pay them for making their beds and other menial household chores! What is the sense of that? How about none! Obviously, it has never occurred to these parent-equals that Ming the Merciless and the last seat in a lifeboat separate the grown-ups from the people who need to grow up.

A dad once told me that he "likes" being his kids' friend. So what? Being a proper parent requires setting aside what you would rather, under utopian circumstances, do for your kids and doing what is best for them. Children do not need thirty- or forty-something buddies. They need firm, calm, constant, loving authority in their lives. That authority cannot come from someone who is trying to be a friend. Friends don't tell friends what they can do, cannot do, and must do.

"Are you saying I should never have fun with my kids?" the same dad asked.

"Not at all," I replied. "Trying to be their friend is trying to be liked. Have fun. Just don't try to be liked. Be the adult in the room. In the long run, they will respect and like you even more."

The job of parent is that of taking the chaotic emotional mess that pretty much defines early childhood (it is not called the "terrible" twos for nothing) and create a disciple—someone who will look up to you (respect you), follow your lead (obey you), and take your values with him into adulthood (pattern himself after you). Use Christ as your example. Despite His disciples' many foibles, He loved them with a love unfathomable (John 15:13), but no one who reads the gospels with discernment would ever get the impression Jesus was trying to get His disciples to like Him. God did not take human form to make a few friends. He had a job to do.

Likewise, *you* have a job to do.

FOR PERSONAL PONDERING AND GROUP DISCUSSION

1. To this point in your parenthood, has your primary objective been that of having wonderful relationship with your children? If so, what worldly pressures have pushed you in that direction?
2. If desire for relationship has hampered your ability to provide firm, calm authority (leadership) to your children, what can you begin doing, today, to set the record straight?
3. What are some of Jesus's attributes that have direct application to good parenting? How?

21
THE BEATLES
WERE WRONG

All you need is love, love,
Love is all you need.

—"*All You Need Is Love,*" *The Beatles,*
1967 (Magical Mystery Tour)

For the LORD disciplines the one He loves, and He chastises
everyone He receives as a son.

—*Hebrews 12:6*

Prior to introducing me to an audience gathered at his church on a
Sunday afternoon, a very gracious and well-meaning pastor prayed,
"Lord, bless the parents here today and help them in their efforts to
properly nurture and love their children."

Because I speak mostly in churches, my talks and seminars are
often prayed over, and with rare exception the pastor asks the Lord
to strengthen parental love. I cannot recall a pastor ever praying that
parents be strengthened in their discipline, yet the Bible puts more
emphasis on parental discipline than on parental love. At the least, they
are described—as in Hebrews 12:6—as two sides of the same coin.
Furthermore, it should be obvious that American parents, especially the

sort who attend parenting seminars, do not lack in love for their kids; rather, they lack in a proper attitude toward and approach to discipline.

Furthermore, the parents in my audiences are fully aware that their problems are disciplinary in nature. They are not coming to my seminars looking for advice on how to better nurture their kids; rather, they are coming in the hope that I will help them solve discipline problems. In short, the emphasis assigned to the need for parents to better love their kids is misplaced, however well-intentioned. While researching the history of child rearing in America, I discovered that up until the 1960s, what scant child-rearing advice there was stressed the need for proper discipline. Little was said about the need for parents to love their children. That omission did not reflect a general lack of parental affection; it simply assumed—and correctly so—that parents who did not love their children were unlikely to seek child-rearing advice.

The shift in emphasis from discipline to nurturing took place alongside a parallel shift from training emotional control to properly understanding and responding to children's emotional output. Both shifts occurred in the 1960s and 1970s as American parents began listening to secular parenting experts put primary stress on the need for parents to make children "feel good about themselves," praise lavishly while largely ignoring misbehavior, and let children "express their feelings freely." This radically new set of understandings caused parents to think that since discipline, especially of a punitive sort, did not make children feel good about themselves, it should be avoided. The progressive propaganda worked. Sixty-plus years into this psychological parenting experiment one encounters a shocking number of parents who dispense lots of love but little in the way of effective discipline. Not surprising, then, is the fact that many children lack emotional resilience along with basic respect for authority.

The title of this chapter refers to a song by The Beatles—the number-one hit, "All You Need Is Love," written by Lennon/McCartney and recorded in 1967. The song's refrain is unequivocal: "All you need is love, love, love is all you need." The sentiment is lovely, but when applied to the raising of a child, it fails to take human sin into consideration. Teaching a child to keep his sin nature under control requires both unconditional love *and* unequivocal discipline. The Bible could not be clearer on the fact that righteous discipline and righteous love are inseparable; they go hand in hand. As our heavenly Parent loves and disciplines those He receives as His children, so earthly parents are to both love and discipline their children in equal measure.

So, Lord, help the parents reading this book understand that the Beatles were wrong; love alone is not sufficient to the proper training of Your children. Discipline is surely, and sorely, needed, especially these days. Amen.

FOR PERSONAL PONDERING AND GROUP DISCUSSION

1. Is your discipline of your children as powerful as your expressed love for them, or is the love/discipline equation tilted toward love? If so, what worldly influences have contributed to that lopsidedness?
2. If the love/discipline equation in your household is tilted toward love, what have been the consequences of that lopsidedness to you and your kids?
3. If your love for your kids has been more powerfully expressed than your discipline, what do you intend to do to rebalance the equation?

22
WORKS-BASED PARENTING

Be still, and know that I am God.

—*Psalm 46:10*

God is sovereign over His creation, and unequivocally so. He blesses those who bless Him. He is faithful to those who love Him and trust Him and acknowledge Him in everything they do. He is the source of all mercy and grace. In contemporary vernacular, He is taking care of business, every little bit of it. As a parent, you have a job to do. When all is said and done, it is the simple job of representing God properly to your children. As such, sound child-rearing—beyond guaranteeing the basics of food, water, shelter, and protection—is nothing more than providing for children what God provides us—unconditional love and unequivocal authority. Anything else is window dressing.

Unfortunately for themselves, their children, their communities, and America, too many parents these days are consumed with window dressing. They seem to think that good parenting requires setting up regular playdates beginning in early toddlerhood, throwing lavish birthday parties every twelve months (beginning at twelve months), driving children from one extracurricular activity to another, giving nightly help with homework, and generally doing everything humanly possible to ensure that one's children never suffer frustration, failure, defeat, disappointment, insult, or any of the other setbacks that make for an authentic life. Needless to say (albeit they need to hear it), the parents in question never succeed at this venture because no amount of effort on the part of a child's parents will alter reality.

The parents I am describing cannot be still. They—mothers, mostly, sad to say—seem compelled to be in near-constant child-oriented motion. With a touch of tongue-in-cheek, I call it "parenting OCD." As a mom once confessed to me, "If I sit down during the day with the intention of putting my feet up for a few minutes, I immediately begin to think of things I could and should be doing for my kids." This mom and moms like her have been unwittingly recruited into the Good Mommy Club (see chapter 8). Membership in the GMC requires that a mother devote herself, 24/7, body, soul, heart, and mind to her kids. The Good Mommy has no life she can call her own. The Good Mommy may be married, but she is, in her own mind, a single parent whose child's future depends on *her* devotion, dedication, and doing. Most unfortunately, the Good Mommy is too busy being a Good Mommy to be a good (biblical) wife. In almost every instance, the Good Mommy's husband is nothing more than a parenting aide who requires her direction and supervision to correctly execute even the most mundane parenting task.

The Good Mommy pays as much attention to her kids as she possibly can, does as much for them as she is able, solves every problem that comes up in their lives, and does whatever is possible to make sure they have everything they want and excel at everything they do. Then she complains of how hard it is to raise children, how much work it requires, how exhausting it is, how stressed out she is, how she never has a moment's peace, and so on. When two or more Good Mommies get together, they talk about nothing but their children—the wonderful things they are doing and providing for their children and their children's equally wonderful achievements and life experiences.

No doubt about it, the Good Mommy Club is a works-based cult. The idols being worshipped by its members are their children. As in

Hinduism, each GMC member creates a personal idol and then worships it. Then she creates another idol, and then perhaps even more. The Good Mommy is generally found running frantically from idol to idol, making sure each receives its fair share of daily worship. The idols in question eventually catch on and begin demanding more and more attention, sacrifice, and obedience. If their demands are not met adequately and in a timely fashion, they begin to weep piteously or rage terrifyingly, which is why most GMC members often feel that no matter how much they do, they are falling short of the mark.

The Good Mommy Club is the most destructive thing that has ever happened to women, yet women do not organize marches in protest of it, form chapters of Good Mommies Anonymous, or go on television talk shows and warn other women about its debilitating effects. They just go along with its belittling agenda. Their husbands go along, too, because they have learned that if they say anything that seems the least bit critical of the GMC, they are accused of not understanding (which is true).

I take every opportunity to encourage women to resign from the GMC and develop rich lives of their own apart from their kids (beginning with developing themselves as godly wives). Mothers need recreations, relationships, and responsibilities that are separate and apart from rearing children. I have heard back from a fair number of women who have adopted that sort of minimalist approach to motherhood. Every one of them tells me the same three things: Resigning from the GMC is the most liberating thing they've ever done; they've had to find all new friends (other women who have escaped the GMC prison); and despite the drawbacks, it's been well worth it.

Any worldly commitment, any worldly responsibility that demands one's utmost is idolatry, and idolatry prevents one from truly knowing God. So, when He says, "Be still, and know that I am God," He is not making a mere suggestion. In the whole of His Word, there is not one example of Him submitting to us an idea for casual consideration. He is being quite serious, and believe me, you do not want to challenge Him on this point.

FOR PERSONAL PONDERING AND GROUP DISCUSSION

1. Are you currently an unwitting member of the Good Mommy Club? If so, is there some redeeming aspect of the GMC that prevents you from resigning? What, pray tell?

2. In addition to the GMC doctrine identified above, can you identify other GMC requirements? How about, "The Good Mommy makes sure her children never feel 'different'"?

3. What, if anything, prevents you from being a Psalm 46:10 parent? As in, starting today!

23
NOTHING LESS
THAN WARFARE

For rebellion is as the sin of witchcraft, and stubbornness is as iniquity and idolatry.

—1 Samuel 15:23 (KJV)

For we do not wrestle against flesh and blood, but against the rulers, against the authorities, against the cosmic powers over this present darkness, against the spiritual forces of evil in the heavenly places.

—Ephesians 6:12 (ESV)

The prophet Samuel is talking to Israel's first king, Saul, who has disobeyed God's instructions concerning the taking of spoils after defeating the Amalekites. Not only had Saul allowed his soldiers to plunder and loot from the pagans; he had also allowed their livestock to be offered as sacrifice to Yahweh. Saul's excuse: the people clamored for it. That only made his sin that much worse. Effectively, Saul was admitting that he was more concerned with pleasing his subjects than pleasing God. Saul was the consummate politician. Like a young child, Saul believed that achieving the desired end justifies the means. From the get-go, children are bent toward pride, self-esteem, and self-idolatry. Saul had never outgrown any of those inclinations. Saul behaved like a child, so God treated him as such. He "spanked" him, big time.

Satan is the author of all lies. Everything false, untrue, is of Satan. Witchcraft is the manipulation of perception to create illusions that mimic miracles but are the very opposite. Witchcraft is all about Satan. That, Samuel told Saul (keep in mind that Samuel is acting as God's spokesperson), was the measure of his sin against God. He did not just slip up. He rebelled against the Holy One. What he did was not just out of order. It was downright evil.

Parents are called upon to reflect God's unconditional love and unequivocal authority to their children. Reflecting God's authority means being uncompromising when it comes to the enforcement of standards, instructions, and boundaries. Synonyms of uncompromising include unwavering, intolerant (calmly, not emotionally), steadfast, and resolute. Many if not most parents have great difficulty wrapping their heads around the idea that a child's disobedience is a manifestation of evil—from the beginning, mind you, when the bud of disobedience first appears (around eighteen months, give or take a few). They pass it off as innocent, *sans* intent. That is certainly understandable. After all, when the average person thinks of evil, he thinks Dracula, Hitler, or the Joker, but evil can wear a cute, cherubic face. This is not the same as saying a child is unrefined evil. He is, however, congenitally infected with a sin nature passed along through his ancestral line that every child expresses at times. Those expressions—no matter their quality, quantity, frequency, or intensity—are not accidental, and they are definitely meaningful.

When their children first begin to test their authority, the parents in question are likely to say things like, "Oh, he didn't know what he was doing," "He's just a baby," "He really didn't mean it," and "He must be tired." Explanations of that naïve sort mistake the toddler's inability to explain his motives with an inability to understand what he is doing. They are not one and the same. Understanding does not require language. Even a newborn is thinking, albeit in sensory images. A child begins acting with purposeful intent before his first birthday. A toddler certainly knows what he is doing and is acting with deliberation.

An eighteen-month-old who bites a playmate did so because he wanted the other child's toy or was trying to protect what he regards as *his* territory—in short, there was nothing accidental about it.

To say that a member of the most intelligent species on the planet—even before his second birthday—does not know what he is doing is absurd, and dangerously so. The fact that when asked why he did what he did the toddler answers, "I don't know," is irrelevant. He knows. He simply can't express it. To think less of him insults his intelligence. Inevitably, parents who underestimate a young child's purposefulness and mental acuity put off dealing with misbehavior. Unfortunately, by the time their excuses run out the child's misbehavior is likely to have developed into a rampaging bull elephant.

The Bible clearly says that a child's sinful nature is present and active when the child is born (Psalm 51:5). That sinful nature is constituted primarily of prideful determination to prove that no one is qualified to tell the Almighty I Am—the young child's fantasy of who he is—what to do. And make no mistake, when a young child behaves in some evil way, the author of all evil is nearby, whispering into the child's ear, "You don't have to cow-tow to your parents; they're just trying to keep you from living life to the fullest!" For all those reasons, the discipline of a child is akin to a form of spiritual warfare. The child's rebellion, especially if it is successful, feeds his pride, and pride, constituted of equal parts illusion of self-sufficiency and illusion of self-importance, is idolatry of the most insidious sort.

Proper discipline that is unwavering, calmly intolerant, and resolute is the antidote to a child's penchant toward pride. Proper discipline causes a child to submit, eventually, to his parents' authority. Conversely, improper discipline enables rebellion. Make no mistake, a child's submission to parental authority is in his own best interest. It prepares him for submission to God and the lordship of Christ Jesus. Put bluntly, a child who does not submit to his parents' authority is on his way to becoming a secularist.

Proper, godly discipline is a form of spiritual warfare that parents conduct on a child's behalf. As the apostle Paul made perfectly clear, it is a battle against the cosmic powers over this present darkness, against spiritual forces of evil. There are no two ways about it. Make sure, therefore, before you go into this battle, and primarily for your child's sake, that you are wearing the armor of God. Read His Word. Study it. Pray. Strengthen yourself!

FOR PERSONAL PONDERING AND GROUP DISCUSSION

1. Name five characteristics of godly discipline. Start with "just."
2. What does "calmly intolerant" discipline look like and not look like?
3. How early in your child's life did you first see his or her sin nature express itself? How did you respond? What would you have done differently if you had understood that discipline is a form of spiritual warfare?

24
NO PAIN, NO GAIN

No discipline seems pleasant at the time, but painful. Later on,
however, it produces a harvest of righteousness and peace for
those who have been trained by it.

—Hebrews 12:11 (NIV)

Applied to child-rearing, this scripture could be paraphrased: "If what a
parent *thinks* was discipline did not cause the child emotional discomfort—grief, guilt, remorse—then it was not true discipline and the child
will not profit from it."

Today's parents tend to believe that just as there have been great
technological advances since the 1960s, there have been great advances
in parenting. They believe, in other words, in parenting progressivism—that there are new "parenting things" under the sun. Even many
professing Christians believe in parenting progressivism! Today's parents
also believe in experts (like yours truly). Actually, believing in parenting
progressivism and believing in parenting experts go hand in hand. After
all, the idea that there have been great parenting advances since the
1960s was manufactured by said experts. Unfortunately, these experts
have done a laudable job of selling parents on the new ideas they have
pulled out of thin air (not like yours truly).

When I was in graduate school, married, and the parent of a young and very strong-willed child, the new parenting experts began demonizing traditional forms of discipline. Not some of the forms in question, mind you, but *all* of them—spanking, grounding, taking away privileges, extra chores. If discipline was punitive, they demonized it. According to the experts, traditional forms of discipline imparted pain to children, emotionally and otherwise; therefore, they were bad, even abusive. Children could be reasoned with, they claimed, and on those rare occasions when a consequence was called for, a few minutes sitting in a comfortable upholstered chair would suffice.

Most of the parents who were buying into this lie had experienced discomforting discipline as children. They remembered not liking it, nearly always thinking it was somehow unfair. By the way, in case you haven't noticed, *children don't like being disciplined.* It was, therefore, relatively easy to sell young parents like my wife and me—who looked back on these discomforting experiences with eyes that were not yet fully adult—on the idea that painless discipline, such as explaining, reasoning, time-out (as long as the chair was upholstered), was loving, whereas discipline of the sort they had experienced as kids was not.

And so off down the road of pain-free discipline went American parents, following the Pied Pipers of *all you need is love.* The outcome of this progressive experiment in child discipline has been a disaster. Child well-being is lower than it has ever been, and parent stress is higher than it has ever been. The experts, loathe to admit they were wrong, have responded to a problem they created by inventing various diagnoses (e.g., attention deficit hyperactivity disorder, oppositional defiant disorder, intermittent explosive disorder, bipolar disorder of childhood), none of which are indicative of anything except children stuck in the throes of toddlerhood (which adherence to *nouveau* parenting doctrine makes virtually inevitable). The mental health professions invented these fake diagnoses to avoid responsibility for the debacle their advice had unleashed. The experts then tell parents that pain-free discipline is even more essential to the well-being of children they diagnose. And so, the kids they "treat" rarely get better, and a good percentage get worse.

The upshot of this pseudo-scientific propaganda is that many of today's parents practice what I call "yada-yada discipline." They respond to their children's sinfulness by talking, and talking, and talking, and more talking. This yada-yada begets nothing but more anarchy, which is why said parents often describe themselves as "screamers." They say they yell and scream because their kids are "difficult" and "strong-willed." Not so. They are yelling and screaming because they are talking when they should be acting. You cannot talk a child out of his sin condition. After talking and accomplishing nothing, they yell. And because yelling accomplishes nothing, they eventually throw their hands in the air, take their kids to mental health professionals, and get disinformation, fake diagnoses, and drugs with dangerous side effects.

Per the theme of chapter 23, the discipline of a child is a form of spiritual warfare conducted on behalf of the child by his parents, who are acting as God's surrogates. That is a serious assignment, as Satan is the face behind all sin. He is the author of deceit and disobedience. Parents would do well to accept that Satan will not be talked out of trying to recruit a child into his malevolent service—yes, even *your* child.

FOR PERSONAL PONDERING AND GROUP DISCUSSION

1. Have you tried to discipline your children without causing pain, much less mere discomfort? If so, what have been the consequences of that well-intentioned attempt?
2. Spanking is not the only way to cause a misbehaving child corrective pain; in fact, it may be, in the long run, the *least* effective way (chapter 13). What are several forms of "painful" discipline that can be effectively used in lieu of physical punishment?
3. Are you resistant to causing your child emotional distress when he misbehaves? If so, why?

25
FALSE TEACHINGS

For the time will come when people will not put up with sound
doctrine. Instead, to suit their own desires, they will gather
around them a great number of teachers to say what their
itching ears want to hear.

—*2 Timothy 4:3 (NIV)*

It goes without saying, false teachings are, well, false, but the most effective false teachings are also very *clever* in that they have significant "curb appeal." At first reading or hearing, there is a quality to many a false teaching that tickles the ear. The teaching in question sounds good, even biblically truthful. When people hear a cleverly phrased false teaching, they are likely to nod their heads, nudge one another, and remark on how gifted the speaker is. Another clever aspect of many false teachings is they are often sprinkled in among true teachings. In that case, the listener is already nodding his head and just keeps right on nodding as the speaker switches from truth to falsehood and then back to truth again. Further compounding the problem of false teachings is that the people who dispense them are often unwitting. They are convinced they are speaking truth, and their own conviction enables them to convince, and therefore mislead, others.

The popular Christian parenting adage, "Rules without relationship leads to rebellion," is a good example of a false teaching that tickles the ear. Primarily because of its almost poetic use of alliteration, it has instant allure. To my knowledge, this particular adage has not been examined critically (until now) because it is found embedded in teachings that are otherwise full of wisdom, which simply proves that not even the wisest of men is without error. "Rules without relationship lead to rebellion" has led many a parent to believe that their primary goal should be to strive for delightful relationship with their kids; that a warm, affectionate, communicative (palsy-walsy, touchy-feely, smoochy-coochie—I could go on, but I'll stop there for the reader's sake) parent–child relationship will prevent all manner of discipline problems. In that case, the rather prominent folks who are pushing this notion need to explain why discipline problems (outward rebellion in various forms) have increased exponentially as more and more parents since the 1960s have put relationship first. That incontestable fact can only be explained thus: When parents put relationship first, they seriously handicap their ability to provide much-needed leadership (authority) to their children. As I have already said (but it bears repeating), it is impossible to discipline effectively when you want the person you are "disciplining" to like you.

Since the aphorism became popular in Christian parenting circles, I have been taking an ongoing poll of people around my age—people raised for the most part in the 1950s. It consists of three questions:

1. Were you, as a child, fundamentally obedient or defiant and rebellious?
2. Looking back on your childhood, do you think your parents were trying to have and sustain a wonderful relationship with you?
3. Did you, as a child, have what you consider a decent and adequate relationship with your parents?

At least 90 percent of the Baby Boomers in this informal survey tell me they were fundamentally obedient children. As for the second question, I have yet to find someone my age who thinks his or her parents were striving primarily for wonderful relationship. In fact, most of my respondents smile—some even laugh—at the idea. "Not in the least, John," is the typical answer. In the 1950s and before, the adult male in the family was a husband first, a father second. Likewise, the adult female was a wife first, a mother second. That is the arrangement in accord with God's plan (see chapter 2). It goes a long way toward explaining the relatively low divorce rate in the 1950s. As for whether people my age think they had a "decent and adequate relationship" with their parents, the overwhelming majority answer in the affirmative.

So much for "rules without relationship lead to rebellion." It simply is not true. Making and enforcing rules is a parental responsibility. Furthermore, when parents let children know that when a rule is made it will be enforced, consistently and dispassionately, it *prevents* rebellion; it does not *cause* it. Most rules describe boundaries. In His Word, God describes lots of boundaries. The first of God's boundaries involved a certain tree. Up to the point of describing that boundary, God was apparently having a great relationship with His first two children. That relationship was "up close and personal," in fact. The garden was home to Adam and Eve, but it was God's earthly home as well. When He was not in heaven, God was communing with Adam and Eve in "Paradise Shores Resort."

Then, one day, God turned his back just long enough for the serpent—not a snake, mind you, but a exceptionally clever being—to make Adam and Eve an offer they did not refuse. They disobeyed. Mind you, they disobeyed a Parent who had created them for the primary purpose of having—pay attention!—*relationship* with them. At that tragic point, God realized that His children didn't take Him seriously and were in need of firm discipline. He realized, in fact, that if He was ever going to restore a proper relationship with them, He had to focus primarily on training them up in the way they should go (Prov. 22:6, chapter 11). So, He promptly emancipated them and began their discipline. Ever since, God's discipline—chastisement, rebuke, correction, and punishment—has been conspicuous in our experience of Him as our Father in heaven.

It simply is not true that relationship prevents rebellion. The more accurate adage is, "Relationship without first having established the rules and demonstrating one's calm determination to enforce them opens the door wide to rebellion and lots of heartache for parents." That's not as pithy, obviously, as "rules without relationship ..." which is why it's not going to become well-known and oft quoted, no matter how truthful it is.

It must be said, however, that anything can be carried to an extreme, and rules are no exception. Although rules are essential to proper parenting, a point is reached where they begin to create more problems than they solve. That is known as "the point of diminishing returns." When parents exceed that limit, they begin to micromanage, and micromanagement almost always leads to rebellion. Sometimes the rebellion is overt; sometimes it is covert.

It cannot be overstressed: The two biggest of all parent obligations are to provide unconditional love and unequivocal leadership. To unconditionally love a child does not require a delightful, fun-filled relationship. It simply means that—as is the case with God's love for us incorrigibles—your love for your child is constant even as his obedience swings wildly and randomly up and down. Most people who read books of this sort not only love their kids unconditionally but also love them more than they love themselves. If you would sacrifice your life to save your child's, then the preceding statement is true of you. Your love is unconditional, and your love of your child greatly exceeds your love of yourself. But, again, neither of those conditions require that you have a delightful, fun-and-games relationship with your child.

Furthermore, a truly great relationship is only possible between two people who are both equally invested in having one. This may be disillusioning to some readers, but children are incapable of investing equally in having a great relationship with their parents. Said another way, you cannot have a great relationship with a person who is not your moral equal, and your child is not your moral equal. That is not arguable. You would give up the last seat in the lifeboat for your child, but your child is not going to give up that same seat for you—no way! Maybe he would at age thirty-five, but he's not going to give it up for you when he's five or ten or even fifteen. That proves, beyond a shadow of doubt, that your child is not your moral equal. Therefore, it is *impossible* for you to have a truly delightful relationship with your child. Trying to have such a relationship requires that you do all the work, which defines a one-sided relationship, and one-sided relationships are not wonderful, except maybe for one of the parties involved.

The further problem is that the attempt to have wonderful relationship all but completely cancels a parent's ability to discipline effectively. As any effective leader will testify, wonderful relationship gets in the way of leadership. But the equal truth is that proper leadership eventually leads to proper relationship. That is attested to by an overwhelming majority of us Baby Boomers. As the Bible says, "To everything there is a season, and a time to every purpose under Heaven" (Ecclesiastes 3:1, chapter 8). In the raising of a child, there is a time for leadership and a time for relationship. Keeping those seasons in their proper order is of benefit to all concerned.

FOR PERSONAL PONDERING AND GROUP DISCUSSION

1. Consider that if you are having significant disciplinary difficulties— if your child is disobedient, disrespectful, and ungrateful—that you may be prioritizing relationship over leadership, wanting your child to like you. In that event, ask yourself how the attempt at relationship is expressing itself in your parenting behavior. Are you, for example, "pulling your disciplinary punches" because you don't want your child to ever be upset with you?
2. Once you have identified the problem, decide how you're going to go about solving it. Do you, for example, need to pay more attention to and spend the majority of your "down" time with your spouse? That, in fact, is the best of all places to start putting things in your family back in proper order.
3. Referencing chapter 8, when does the Season of Relationship begin?

26

FALSE TEACHINGS, PART TWO

"Beware of false prophets, who come to you in sheep's clothing but inwardly are ravenous wolves."

—*Matthew 7:15*

In the Sermon on the Mount, Jesus warns of false prophets who will appear to be genuine, Spirit-filled teachers of the gospel but in fact will be "ravenous wolves" who lead credulous people to destruction. Elsewhere, Jesus becomes even more specific, telling his disciples that the false prophets in question will come in His Name (Matt. 24:5).

In response to the term "false prophets," the typical twentieth-century believer is likely to think in terms of certain well-known mega-church pastors who claim to represent Christ but promote a false prosperity gospel or televised revival preachers who perform bogus faith healings by high-fiving people's foreheads while shouting "Heah-lah!" in a backwoods accent. Indeed, some false prophets occupy positions of influence in the contemporary Christian world, but people who misrepresent God's Word to mean something it does not mean are by no means limited to self-promoting mega-church pastors and tent-show faith healers. The following story is illustrative.

After a talk on biblical parenting that I gave at a Southern Baptist church in North Carolina, a mother tried to draw me into an argument by accusing me of promoting an approach to child-rearing that did not reflect Jesus's mercy and grace. She claimed I was advocating an "Old Testament view" of the sin nature of children and claimed that "Jesus came to change all that."

According to her, the God of the Old Testament was angry, punitive, and unforgiving. Obedience to the Old Testament God was fear-based. Jesus, on the other hand, was all about grace, love, and forgiveness. Jesus, not the Old Testament God, was her parenting role model. She talked as if the God of Hebrew scripture and Jesus were two completely different persons; as if Jesus came to correct the mistakes His hotheaded Father had made. She obviously did not possess a well-informed theology; nonetheless, my curiosity was piqued. I asked her to identify the primary source of her approach to child rearing.

"Grace-based parenting," she answered, proudly.

At the time, I was but superficially familiar with Tim Kimmel's best-selling book and program of the same name. My initial impression was skeptical. Several older pastors had told me they were troubled by it. Grace-based parenting appeared to them to be nothing more than a pseudo-biblical repackaging of postmodern psychological parenting. In addition, several moms had told me that discovering my writings had saved them from child-rearing disasters brought on by following Kimmel's advice. I decided, however, that I needed more than hearsay to understand where Kimmel was coming from and promoting. So, I perused his website and read his book, *Grace-Based Parenting,* discovering in the process that Kimmel commits a good amount of theological error.

To begin with, he contrasts grace-based parenting with what he terms "legalistic" parenting. Hopelessly rule-oriented parents, according to Kimmel, "do their best to create an environment that controls as many of the avenues as possible that sin could use to work its way into the inner sanctum ... as though the power to sin or not to sin was somehow connected to their personal will power and resolve." Indeed, there are parents who think sufficient vigilance will prevent their children from sinning. But creating a home environment that minimizes a child's exposure to sinful influences is one of a parent's primary responsibilities. That effort is not, in and of itself, legalistic, nor is it necessarily indicative of a parent who believes he or she is the ultimate source of her child's salvation. When Jesus said, "if your eye causes you to sin, gouge it out" (Mark 9:47), he was not saying you can save yourself from sin. He was saying that if you identify a source of sin in your life, you should eliminate it, no matter the immediate personal cost. Because children are not capable of reliably identifying and eliminating sources of sin in their lives, parents must stand ready to perform that function on their behalf. That is not legalism; it is responsible parenting.

Kimmel claims that grace-based parents "don't bother spending much time putting fences up because they know full well that sin is already present and accounted for inside their family." But the fact that sin is a human condition does not mean parents should not be proactive about putting up fences between their children and spiritually and morally corrupting influences. Yes, parents can overdo putting up such fences, but attempting to minimize untoward influence is a parent's biblical responsibility. Not providing children with smart phones and video games, not allowing girls to wear provocative clothing, establishing and enforcing reasonable curfews, not allowing extracurricular activities to overwhelm the family—that is a short list of "fences" that parents should erect and maintain. Doing so is not legalistic or lacking in grace; it is responsible parenting.

Kimmel says parents who lack grace insist that their children behave properly and punish them when they do not: "The graceless home requires kids to be good and gets angry and punishes them when they are bad." Granted, punishment should not be driven by anger, but punishing a child for purposeful misbehavior is essential to moral instruction. When the author of Hebrews says proper discipline is not "pleasant at the time, but painful" (12:11, chapter 24), he is speaking of punishment. The same is true of Hebrews 12:6: *For the Lord disciplines the one he loves, and chastises every son whom he receives ... for what son is there whom his father does not discipline?*" Make no mistake about it, the words *chastises* and *discipline* as used in this verse are unmistakable synonyms for punishment. In short, Kimmel's take on punishment is theologically indefensible.

What is Kimmel's solution to a child's misbehavior? He says that grace-based parents, instead of punishing when sin occurs, help their kids "learn how to tap into God's power to help them get stronger." What does that mean? And just how is a parent to go about helping, say, a rebellious, tantrum-throwing four-year-old "tap into God's power"? Repeatedly, Kimmel issues platitudes that sound lovely but are impossible to translate into action. In this case, the Bible is devoid of support for the notion that a human being—regardless of age or belief—is capable of "tapping into God's power." Prayer calls upon God but the notion that through prayer an individual can actually draw power from God is heterodox. Even if that were possible, it is completely unrealistic to think one can teach a raging, defiant four-year-old that he is giving in to sin and needs to tap into God's power to fight the good fight against Satan.

Ecclesiastes 3:1 teaches that there is a "season" for every purpose under heaven, and yes, a time will come in the life of a child when said child will be able to wrap his head around the reality of his sin condition and learn to depend upon the Holy Spirit (through prayer and Bible study) when tempted to sin. But to call upon and rely on and to "tap into" are two entirely different matters.

It did not take much research for me to conclude that grace-based parenting does not accurately represent God's parenting design. Instead of starting with God's Word and helping parents understand how to properly apply it, Kimmel has started with his own ideas and attempted to shoehorn them into God's Word. He certainly doesn't qualify as a "ravenous wolf"; nonetheless, some of his core teachings, as linguistically appealing as they might be, are not supported by the Bible's plain text.

The essential foundations of proper, effective discipline are set between a child's second and third birthdays, approximately. What parents accomplish or, as may be the case, fail to accomplish during that critical year will significantly affect whether the child's discipline will be a relatively simple matter or difficult and frustrating from that point on. A child of that age is simply incapable of making an informed proclamation of Christ and will not be able to do so for several years to come at best. Until then, dealing with the sin nature of a child requires firm, unequivocal authority that involves rules and boundaries—what Kimmel unfortunately and wrongly refers to as legalisms. Furthermore, the discipline in question will require—not *may*, but *will*—punishment, which is a valid means of parents properly imaging God's authority.

Kimmel is a good salesman. Whether he is a good theologian is another question entirely.

FOR PERSONAL PONDERING AND GROUP DISCUSSION

1. What are the characteristics that define a false parenting prophet? Does the term only apply to someone who wittingly leads parents astray?
2. What similarities do grace-based parenting and postmodern psychological parenting have in common?
3. How does it benefit a child for his parents to punish his misbehavior? What does Hebrews 12:11 mean by saying that proper discipline produces a "harvest of righteousness and peace for those who have been trained by it" (NIV)?

27
LOVE UNCONDITIONAL

For all have sinned and fall short of the glory of God, and all are justified freely by his grace through the redemption that came by Christ Jesus.

—Romans 3:23–24

There is a lot of talk in the Christian world about unconditional love, but what, exactly, is it? Answer: *Unconditional love is God's love.* Only God can love without condition, prerequisite, or expectation—with nothing more than grace, hope, and faithfulness. Human beings may talk about loving unconditionally, but human beings are incapable of more than approximating what it means to love without condition, prerequisite, or expectation. Because of our congenital sin condition, 100 percent unconditional love is not in our wheelhouse. And yes, sorry to say, the foregoing applies to our love for our children. In our parenting, we can but approximate God's love. Maybe this will help: God is Holy with a capital H. In everything we humans do, no matter how hard we try, no matter our intentions, we fall way, way short of His glory and Holiness. That is why we cannot be justified by works. Sin cannot purge itself any more than dirt can make itself clean. We can only be justified "by His grace through the redemption that came by Christ Jesus ."

So, when we sinful humans speak of loving our children uncondi-tionally, it is a boast, an overstatement. That's the bad news. The good news, however, is that the kind of parent who reads books of this sort—*you*, in other words—already comes as close as is humanly possible to God's Holy standard. Would you give your life to save your child's? Of course! (There are parents who would not make that sacrifice, but the parents in question do not read books of this sort.) You would make that decision in a heartbeat and execute it without fear or trepidation! That is what Jesus, out of unconditional love, did for all of us! He even said He would (John 15:13). No doubt about it, you love your child about as unconditionally as is possible for an unholy human! For purposes of this discussion, then, we will bypass the "about as" and just say that your love for your child is unconditional.

Children need their parents' unconditional love—love that is not based on their works—for the same reason we need God's uncondi-tional love. Children are sinful; they are born with a nature that inclines them toward self-love and idolatry of all sorts. During his early years, a child has no idea he is sinful. But as his conscience begins to form, he becomes more and more aware of his sin condition. As that awareness matures, the child becomes increasingly capable of feelings of guilt and remorse.

If parent love was conditional, if it depended on children's works, a lot of children would receive very little love. That is why a parent's love for a child *must* be unqualified, absolute, and not dependent on any action on the child's part. One way a parent demonstrates unconditional love is by acting appropriately when the child misbehaves. The parent (a) reprimands, (b) punishes justly, and then (c) forgives. That three-step process brings about repentance. Actually, that's not exactly true. Step (c)—forgiveness—brings about repentance. If parental discipline stops at (b), it is may succeed at being corrective, but probably only temporarily so. It will not penetrate further than skin deep. Because you (c) forgive, your child knows he is loved and unconditionally so. Telling your child ten times a day that you love him does not begin to measure up to one act of forgiveness on your part. But don't forget steps (a) and (b)!

FOR PERSONAL PONDERING AND GROUP DISCUSSION

1. Are you as good at forgiving as you are at reprimanding, punishing, and seeing the punishment through to the end?
2. Do you avoid punishing your child when he has purposefully done something wrong? If yes, why?
3. Explain why discipline is not likely to "take" if forgiveness is not part of the equation.

28
MONKEY, MONKEY, WHO'S GOT THE MONKEY?

To the woman he said, "I will make your pains in childbearing very severe; with painful labor you will give birth to children… To Adam he said, "Because you listened to your wife and ate fruit from the tree about which I commanded you, 'You must not eat from it,' cursed is the ground because of you. Through painful toil you will eat food from it all the days of your life."

—Genesis 3:16–17 (NIV)

Sigmund Freud, the so-called Father of Modern Psychology (1856–1939), was the first philosopher on record to propose that parenting produced the person, that any given individual began life like a ball of clay that was then shaped into an adult by the actions of his parents. Freud possessed a dismal view of humanity. He thought, for example, that everyone was to some degree mentally ill. In other words, he believed every parent is a bad parent. Like I said, dismal. At the time, his deterministic proposition was radical. It effectively denied both the sovereignty of God and man's free will—no surprise there, given that Freud was an outspoken atheist who regarded belief and faith in a Supreme Being as a form of psychosis.

Freud was also what today would be termed a chauvinist or sexist. He minimized the influence of fathers and pointed his cigar-stained finger of blame for nearly every individual fault and failure at mothers. In his view, mothers rejected their daughters and tried to seduce their sons, and no, I'm not kidding. Notwithstanding the bizarre nature of his theories, but primarily because they were radically *nouveau* and European, Freud's writings gained traction in America's universities and their influence spread from there. By the early 1960s, his bizarre ideas had permeated popular culture. The new parenting experts that began arising in the late 1960s—most of whom were psychologists and other mental health professionals—incorporated Freud's wacky ideas into their theories and advice. As a result, the American mother began to think she was the sole determining factor in her child's life, that whether her child developed problems of any sort—behavioral, emotional, social, academic—was entirely up to her. Freud is why so many contemporary moms, when something goes awry in their children's lives, become beset with anxiety and guilt.

After describing some moral flaw on her adult child's part, a guilt-beset mom asks, "What did I do wrong?" In fact, said mom has done a number of wrong things, as has every parent throughout history. Even if she has always acted from good intent, she has done dumb, unthinking, counterproductive, self-defeating things. So has her husband. This being a broken world and everyone being sinful, that is simply the way things are. Knowing that, God instilled a good amount of resiliency, emotional and otherwise, into human beings. Unlike, say, dogs, human beings, even as children, can bounce back from lots of bad stuff, and the younger they are, the better they bounce.

But the pertinent question is whether the wrong things done by a mother have *caused* her child to commit moral error. Is she to blame for the fact that her child is a bully, disruptive in class, or a lazybones? She has played a role in all of that, certainly, but *blame* is a different matter. Maybe she could have done something different and brought about a different outcome, but that is entirely speculative. Parenting is an influence. It is not, however, reliably deterministic. Because he possesses free will, a child is capable of things that cannot be explained in terms of how he was or is being raised. That goes in both directions, by the way. A child raised by moral, God-fearing people may be more of a problem than a child raised by sociopathic deviants. That is not likely, mind you, but it is possible. It has happened to God, even. The one and only perfect Parent created two children who, as soon as His back was turned, committed the single most egregious and self-destructive act of all time. Needless to say, God's parenting was not the precipitating factor.

When His first kids broke His impeccable moral law, did God wallow in paralyzing guilt? Nope. He kicked them out of his "house." He emancipated them, right there, right then. They did the worst thing they could have done. God, being perfectly just, acted in kind. Did humankind learn its lesson? Nope. We have been carrying the serpent's water ever since, some of us more reliably than others. Likewise, sometimes children learn the lessons provided them; sometimes, however, their oppositional nature rules.

Upon the disobedience of His first two children, God put the monkey of responsibility squarely on their backs. In that metaphor, the monkey represents the emotional and tangible consequences to those first children of their betrayal. It is axiomatic that the monkey of a problem should reside on the back of the person or persons who created the problem. The monkey represents responsibility. Responsibility for a problem—experienced as guilt, for example—is both instructive and motivating. It instructs the person as to the seriousness of the problem and motivates the person to correct his ways. It is also axiomatic that if the monkey is on the back of a person other than the wrongdoer, then the wrongdoer learns nothing and is likely to commit the same error again. So, when a child commits a moral error and one or both of his parents allow the monkey to cling to their backs in the form of guilt, emotional agitation, or attempts on their part to solve a problem their child created, the child is blessed with neither instruction nor corrective motivation. Thus, he is likely to commit the same or a similar moral error again, and again, and again, and he is not likely to stop until the monkey is transferred to his back and he is forced to tame it.

No parent, ever, has endured more heartache because of children than God. If you think you can do better than He has done, best of luck!

FOR PERSONAL PONDERING AND GROUP DISCUSSION

1. Have you taken on the monkey for certain of your child's misdeeds? Have there been or are there still instances when he does something bad and *you* agonize over it?

2. If so, consider that if *you* feel bad about bad things *he* does, the bad things in question will continue to happen and probably worsen over time. ("Give 'em an inch, and they will take a mile.") Shifting that emotional responsibility—the "monkey" of the problem—from your back to your child's may be difficult, but it is the right, kind, and just thing to do. What do you need to do to give your child his monkey(s)?

3. There is nothing that a child appreciates less than a parent who puts a well-deserved monkey on his back. How are you going to deal with your child's reaction when you do exactly that?

29
BECAUSE YOU SAY SO!

Children, obey your parents in the Lord, for this is right.

—*Ephesians 6:1*

While searching for a new church home, my wife and I happened upon a community that had been highly recommended by several folks who seemed to understand what sort of church we were seeking, our first and foremost requirement being a pastor who was expository and adhered to a straightforward reading of the Word.

When we arrived, we were greeted and introduced to the pastor—I'll call him Robert. His first question was "What do you do, John?"

When I told him that I wrote and spoke on raising children, he said, "Oh, my goodness! I hope you approve of my sermon today—it's on parenting."

During the sermon, Pastor Robert drifted further and further from properly exegeting God's child-rearing design—in fact, he was not being expository in the least. Within minutes, it became obvious to me that his parenting philosophy was not biblical; it was Robertian.

The final straw was when he said, "I don't think parents should ever say *because I said so*. Children deserve to know why their parents make the decisions they make."

I leaned over toward my wife and whispered, "That's the dealbreaker, right there."

Willie simply nodded her head.

In his instruction to children in Ephesians, Paul could not be clearer: Children are to obey their parents not because they give an acceptable explanation, offer a sufficiently enticing reward, or threaten a sufficiently scary punishment, but simply because it is right. Paul uses the phrase "in the LORD" to mean that children should obey their parents as if they were obeying God Himself. As explicated elsewhere in this book, parents are to represent God to their children. God does not explain Himself. He simply declares, instructs, and commands. Explanations tend to sound persuasive, and persuasion is not authoritative. As such, explanations tend to arouse a child's defiant nature. In response, the child attempts to deconstruct the parent's explanation. He attempts to entrap the parent in an argument in which the parent tries, usually in vain, to justify his or her decision to the child.

The moment a parent engages in argument with a child, the parent has lost. How? Because the child defines the terms of the exchange. Every time the parent responds to a statement of opposition—a "but!"— from the child, the parent loses more ground. Furthermore, parent-child arguments advance Satan's purposes. Every rebellious act on the part of a child is pleasing to him, and it is doubly pleasing to him when parents enable a child's rebelliousness by arguing.

Pastor Robert was wrong; when it comes to their parents' decisions and commands children do not *deserve* explanations. They *deserve* parents who act in their best interests. We are to obey God simply because He says so. Likewise, children are to obey their parents simply because they say so. End of story.

FOR PERSONAL PONDERING AND GROUP DISCUSSION

1. Have you, to this point, felt that you did not have a right to say "Because I said so" to your kids? If so, can you identify the source of that belief?

2. How do you think your children will respond if you begin using "Because I said so" as a stock reply to "why" and "why not"? What will you say or do in that event?

3. Do you describe your kids as argumentative? What have you done to enable the arguments in question? Are you willing to accept full responsibility for them? (Because if you do not, then they are not going to stop.)

30
THE NARROW PARENTING GATE

"Enter by the narrow gate. For the gate is wide and the way is easy that leads to destruction, and those who enter by it are many. For the gate is narrow and the way is hard that leads to life, and those who find it are few."

—*Matthew 7:13–14*

A fellow once tried to lure me into an argument by accusing me of writing and talking as if there is only one proper way to raise a child.

"That's true," I said. "There is only one proper way."

"Oh, that's truly absurd!" he bellowed. "There are many equally worthwhile ways to parent properly!"

"But," I pointed out, "the various ways you're referring to are different from one another; therefore, their outcomes are also different. How could they be equal?"

After staring at me for a few pregnant moments, he said, "You're just very narrow-minded," and stormed away.

Little did he know that had he stuck around, I would have agreed with him. I *am* narrow-minded. I have tried broad-mindedness and found it severely lacking. There was a time when I believed in the lie of relativism and its promise of personal liberation. I believed that standards, moral and otherwise, were flexible, subject to time, place, and personal whim. I believed in my capacity to define right and wrong for myself. I believed in shades of gray, what is known as "situational ethics." Then, coming to know Christ and reading God's Word, I began to understand that concerning any undertaking, there is only one proper perspective and only one proper approach—God's.

There is but one way to attain eternal life, for example. It is the Lord's way. Many ways are currently promoted as equally viable, but Jesus tells us that He, and only He, is the way to life. The world wants you to believe that Islam, Buddhism, Hinduism, Wicca, even atheism (as long as the atheist in question is a "nice" person), all lead to the same state of eternal glory. Not so. No matter how "happy" or "fulfilled" an adherent to one of those belief systems may claim to be, they are "easy" roads to destruction.   Likewise, there is only one proper way to raise a child—the Lord's way, as referenced in Paul's letter to the Christian community in Ephesus (Eph. 6:4, chapter 15). He has given parents a concise set of instructions by which to raise His children. As is true of every aspect of His Word, God's child-rearing instructions lack nothing and pertain to all children.

As I said in the Introduction, but it bears repeating: God's parenting instructions are perfect, but human beings are imperfect. Human beings, given a perfect set of instructions, will still do an imperfect job. But they will do a far, far better job than if they follow instructions provided by other imperfect human beings.

The sad fact—one that pastors should address from their pulpits—is that Christian parents, as a group, are experiencing the same parenting problems that secular, humanist parents are experiencing. The only possible explanation for this is that an overwhelming majority of Christian parents follow the parenting fads and fashions of the world. They believe that when it comes to the raising of children, there are new things under the sun (Eccles. 1:9, chapter 17). They may call themselves Christian conservatives, but they are parenting progressives, albeit unwittingly.

When it comes to doing anything, the proper way is God's way, and the proper way is always entered through a narrow gate.

FOR PERSONAL PONDERING AND GROUP DISCUSSION

1. In certain ways, have you unwittingly become a parenting relativist? Have you capitulated to peer pressure to raise your children according to the world's ever-changing norms? In what specific ways are you seeking worldly acceptance for how you are raising your kids?

2. What specific traits distinguish a parenting conservative from a parenting progressive?

3. What can you eliminate, this week, from your parenting behavior and your children's lives, that will straighten your parenting path and aim it more accurately toward God's narrow parenting gate? Smart phones? Video games? Some of their after-school activities? Hovering over your kids' homework? The more you eliminate, the lighter your parenting burden will become, until it is no longer a burden at all!

31

PARENTING TRANSFORMATION

Do not be conformed to this world, but be transformed by the renewal of your mind, that by testing you may discern what is the will of God, what is good and acceptable and perfect.

—*Romans 12:2–3 (ESV)*

The will and the ways of God are not the will and the ways of man. Said differently: God's way and the world's way are two different ways. They are as different as different can be, in fact.

Identifying parents who are conforming to this world in how they raise their children is a simple matter. The female parent is a member in good standing of the Good Mommy Club and the male parent is Buddy Dad. The female parent is set on being the best enabler possible, albeit that is certainly not her take on what she is doing. Within her sphere of operation, she pays as much attention to and does as much as she can for her child, generally devoting herself to ensuring that his life is pain-free. She is almost always in motion, and when she is not in motion, she is on stand-by. Exhaustion is the measure of her martyrdom.

Her "husband"—I put quotes around the word because albeit he lives under the same roof, he views "father" as his primary role—is dedicated to being his child's best friend. Unlike his "wife," however, he keeps a good sense of humor most of the time. He can afford humor because his children's mother is doing all the heavy lifting. He is there to occasionally assist or fill in for her, but she is obviously CEO of parenting. She micromanages nearly every waking moment of her children's lives. She's on top of it all! She micromanages her husband's home life as well. He is, after all, prone to lapses of attention.

Both the GMC mom and the Buddy Dad are in codependent relationships with their kids, but in different ways. Her primary desire is to make everything A-OK for her kids; his is to be liked by and have fun with them. In effect, he has become one of the kids, which is evidenced in the amount of time he spends being their playmate.

The question becomes: Am I describing what goes on in your family? If so—and I give "Sadly, John, yes" an 80 to 90 percent likelihood—then you are yet another example of why Christian parents are having the same parenting problems as parents who are unchurched or merely so-called cultural Christians. When one conforms himself to the world, he reaps what the world is reaping. That is an irrevocable cause-effect relationship.

In the scripture under discussion, Paul says that to receive the fullness of God's blessings, to be fully transformed by Jesus's gift of salvation, a believer must step aside and let the Holy Spirit renew their mind. The process of renewal enables the giftee to begin the trial-and-error of discovering that which "is good and acceptable and perfect." Quite simply, if a parent is raising his or her children according to God's will, according to His training and instruction, then the overall experience will be positive. That individual will not describe his or her parenting life in words like exhausted, frustrated, anxious, guilty, angry, and resentful. Rather, the description will be along the lines of "Oh, it's a joy and a blessing." The parent in question is not joyful and feeling blessed because her kids are making straight-A's or being scouted by Olympic-team coaches, but simply because the natural consequence of conforming oneself to God's will is joy and blessings.

If you realize that you have subscribed to the doctrine of the Good Mommy Club or are a Buddy Dad, then step one is to resign. Renounce your apostasy, repent of your rebellious ways, and open your parenting mind to the transforming power of the Great I Am. It's quite simple, actually.

FOR PERSONAL PONDERING AND
GROUP DISCUSSION

1. Have you and your spouse, to this point, been parenting in step with the world? What have been the specific consequences of that conformity?
2. What specific steps do you need to take to bring your parenting into closer alignment with God's design for the family?
3. How will your children react to that transformation, and how do you plan to deal with their reactions? Best to be proactive than reactive.

32

THE PROBLEM WITH "CHRISTIAN" PARENTING

But be doers of the word, and not hearers only, deceiving yourselves.

—*James 1:22*

When they introduced themselves, one of the host couples at a church where I was speaking told me my books were their "parenting bibles." They were raising their three children, they said, by my advice. They asked if they could take me out to dinner. As we broke bread together, and despite my attempts to steer the conversation in other directions, they continued to enthuse about how much my writings had influenced the way they were raising their kids. I listened politely but kept gently reminding them that "my" advice was not mine at all but based on biblical principles and essentially nothing more than a rearticulation of the typical pre-1960s parents' attitude and practice.

After dinner, they invited me to their home where it became evident that they were not really raising their children according to biblical principles, much less what they referred to as "my" advice. Their kids had no chores to speak of, for example. They had a full-time housekeeper who picked up after the kids and even made their beds every

155

morning. When they took me on a tour, I noted that each child's bedroom featured both a computer and a television set and that their son's television was connected to a video game console. All three of the children's bedrooms were stuffed with stuff, and very expensive-looking stuff to boot. Shelves in the oldest daughter's room—she was in the fifth grade at the time—were lined with a collection of porcelain dolls, each dressed to the hilt in designer doll apparel. Numerous trophies for participation in various athletic activities were displayed in a glass trophy case in the den, and professional photos of the children hung in nearly every room of the home. As we talked, they allowed their children to interrupt our conversation at will, never correcting them when they did so.

This was not the first time, nor the last, that I have encountered parents who have told me they raise their children according to Christian or biblical principles along with my advice, but the truth is, they raise their children in keeping with current child-rearing fashions. Their parenting is not informed by Scripture as much as it is informed by the world. I used to puzzle over this phenomenon. Then I happened across the verse in James's epistle (1:22) in which he addresses people who hear and even recite God's Word but do not live their lives in accord with it. In contemporary vernacular, James is referring to Christians who fail to "walk their talk." Every attentive Christian has met fellow churchgoers of this sort—people who reference Scripture liberally but are wanting when it comes to practice. They are gossips, perhaps, or maybe they show off their expensive possessions and brag about their many accomplishments. Whatever, their pious words fail to align with their day-to-day behavior.

Reading James's warning, I realized that some folks read my writings, approve of them, and even enthusiastically recommend them to others but don't actually do much more than read and recommend. They are well-intentioned, for sure. They are not purposefully misrepresenting themselves. James nails it. They are deceiving themselves, and people who are deceiving themselves are not aware of the deception. They convince themselves that reading, approving, and enthusiastically recommending is the same as doing. The psychological term for this is denial.

Their denial is understandable. James does not say so, but strongly implies that being a doer of God's Word is a lot more demanding than simply being a reader of God's Word. Being a doer of the Word requires swimming against the tides of the world, sticking out like a sore thumb, marching to the beat of a different drummer, and the like. In the eyes of the world, people who truly live their lives in accord with God's Word are somewhat odd. They're even odd in the eyes of some regular churchgoers. Odd parents do not put their children center-stage in their lives. They don't brag about their children's accomplishments or the lengths to which they go to support their children's amazing (according to them, at least) talents. Odd parents insist that their children behave properly and firmly enforce their expectations. The boldly authoritative way in which they correct their children can even make other parents uncomfortable. The children of odd parents have more chores than after-school activities. After high school, and regardless of their grades, the children of odd parents are more likely to attend a small Christian college than a top-rated secular university.

Over the years, a fair number of these odd parents have shared their child-rearing experience with me. Almost always, they talk about how difficult it is for them to relate to parents who are not odd—parents who are in the seductive grip of the world—and how generally difficult it is for them to find like-minded parents, even in their churches. Nonetheless, I have never encountered an odd parent who would have it any other way. They would not trade being regarded as odd for being accepted into the parenting mainstream.

If sin is rebellion against God, then it is sinful for Christians to raise their children according to worldly fashions. Unless for whatever reasons other options are non-starters, Christians should not send their children to public schools, for example. Christian parents should not participate in the after-school activities rat race (albeit the occasional after-school activity here and there is fine). Christian children should be expected to help in significant ways with housework. Christian parents should be diligent in teaching their children proper manners and a biblical worldview. There is no better way for parents to express their faith.

FOR PERSONAL PONDERING AND
GROUP DISCUSSION

1. On a scale of 1 to 10, how would you rate your alignment with God's parenting plan versus the world's parenting fashions, where 10 is complete, 100 percent alignment with God's plan?

2. Assuming you did not give yourself a 10, what about the way you are raising your children needs to be brought into closer alignment with God's plan? (Can you and are you willing to identify your parenting sins?)

3. Can you identify fears and anxieties that are holding you captive to the ongoing worldly parenting parade?

33
NOTHING TO FEAR
BUT FEAR ITSELF

Be anxious for nothing, but in everything by prayer and
supplication, with thanksgiving, let your requests be made
known to God; and the peace of God, which surpasses all
understanding, will guard your hearts and minds through
Christ Jesus.

—Philippians 4:6–7

The mother of a seven-year-old boy sent me an email in which she
described her son as smart, motivated, athletic, and well-mannered. He
made good grades in school, did well in sports, and had several close
friends.

"However," she added, "he often allows himself, in sports, to be
intimidated by and taken advantage of by other boys. He is a rule-fol-
lower who worries about getting into trouble if he defends himself. I
worry that other boys will see him as easy to pick on. Occasionally, he
complains about how other boys treat him. What words can I use to
help him be more self-confident and not allow himself to be intimidated
by other boys?"

I just sat, shaking my head. This youngster's well-intentioned mom is
sadly typical. Along with all too many of today's moms, she's anxious,

a compulsive worrier, and strung as tight as a piano wire—not because children *per se* merit anxiety, worrying, and stress, but because today's all-too-typical mom is obsessively fixated on her kids. She puts them under a microscope and searches the details for a problem. If she can't find a problem that justifies her anxiety, worrying, and stress, she invents one to fill the vacuum.

Her husband does not obsess, worry, or stress over the kids much if at all. His lack of worry simply convinces her that he doesn't get it. He is obviously a parenting doofus who requires supervision and direction lest he blunder into the parenting apple cart she can be found carefully arranging and scatters the apples everywhere, requiring her, therefore, to start over again. Mind you, her parenting OCD has nothing to do with being a woman. Her female ancestors did not fit this description—not in the least. This is new stuff.

What brought it about? Psychology, that's what. The psychological parenting theory that "experts" pulled out of the thin air of secular humanism beginning in the 1960s (and have been pulling ever since) emphasized the necessity of understanding and properly responding to a child's feelings. In effect, it legitimated a child's feelings—the "foolishness" that the authority of scripture tells us is characteristic of children (Prov. 22:15, chapter 12). Prior to this, parents understood that a child's feelings are often (but not always) nothing more than chaotic expressions of his irrational nature. Pre-1960s parents understood that as do a child's behavior and thought processes, a child's emotional expressions require proper training. Suddenly, post-1960s, the child's feelings became the barometer by which parents could supposedly know whether they were doing a good job.

It is a given that women are more feeling-oriented than men, so this new body of psychological theory naturally appealed to women. Initially at least, it did not appeal to men (this has changed somewhat, however, as men have become increasingly convinced that they need to "get in touch with their feminine sides"). Consequently, women began to feel that they were the only gender capable of properly understanding and responding to the now-paramount "emotional needs" of children. Unlike any prior generation of women, they convinced themselves that they alone were responsible for the successful out-come of their respective parenting projects; that their children's futures will rise or fall based exclusively on the quality and quantity of their devotion, understanding, love, and diligent activity. According to the new parenting mythology, the most child-focused mother was the best mother.

And so, mothers swung into high gear. And they began worrying, putting their children under magnifying glasses and searching for any indication that something about their kids might be out of whack or might be in danger of going whacky. And the more they worried, the more they turned up the power of their magnifiers. Today we have moms who cannot leave well enough alone, who cannot count their blessings, who cannot see the child-rearing forest for being so focused on the pattern of veins on each leaf of each individual tree. Thus, we have the mom in question, who cannot be content that her son is well-mannered, has good social skills, and does well in sports and in school. In her anxious estimation, he is not assertive enough; therefore, her latest parenting project becomes that of talking him into being more assertive.

The drawback to her child is that the more his mom worries about him, the more likely it becomes that he will begin worrying about himself. Today's kids, in general, are the objects of tremendous parental concern. I think that has contributed significantly to the post-1960s downturn in child and teen mental health. Parental concern becomes a self-fulfilling prophecy, eventually engendering things that merit genuine concern. This mom needs to follow Paul's advice. Instead of dwelling obsessively and anxiously on the minutiae of parenting, she needs to pray, thanking God for her son's wonderful positives. Paul promises that such prayer will result in God bringing peace through Jesus. Anxiety, after all, is nothing more than the inevitable result of not trusting adequately in God. Anxiety is the result of over-focusing on worldly concerns. It goes without saying that when one is focused on worldly concerns, those concerns will always seem more significant and troublesome than they truly are.

Prayer puts all things in proper perspective.

FOR PERSONAL PONDERING AND
GROUP DISCUSSION

1. Have you over-focused on your children? Are you worried about small imperfections that will probably work themselves out over time? If so, make a list of them and resolve to pray about them, asking God for guidance and peace.

2. Do you give more credence to your children's feelings than they deserve? Have your kids become drama factories? If you now realize that a child's feelings require no less discipline (training) than his behavior and thought processes, what can you do to begin helping your child take more responsibility for his feelings and begin bringing them under control?

3. Compose a prayer of joy and thanksgiving for each of your children's positive qualities. Pray these prayers at least once a day for a week. Don't you feel better already?

34
FOCUS ON THE HORIZON

Where there is no vision, the people perish; but he that keepeth
the law, happy is he.

—*Proverbs 29:18 (KJV)*

This well-known scripture does not mean what heretical prosperity preachers claim. It does not mean that God fulfills the hopes and dreams of
the faithful. Quite the contrary. It means that the Word of God imparts
wisdom and vision; as Jesus put it, "eyes that see" (e.g., Matt. 13:16). Jesus
was referring to people who correctly perceived that He was Messiah, the
Word made flesh as prophesied in scripture. God gave us His special revelation—the Old and New Testaments—that we might know Him more
intimately and live our lives in step with His will. When Jesus identified
Himself as "the Way," He used the definite article *the* to make clear that
He was not one of numerous equally authentic ways, but the one and only
truthful Way that leads to eternal life. In that regard, it is significant that
the disciple John refers to Jesus as "the Word made flesh" (John 1:14).
Jesus is the embodiment of everything God. To accept Him as Lord and
Savior is to "see," to possess wisdom and vision; to reject Him is to "have
eyes that do not see."

Some folks are highly selective when it comes to accepting the truth
of Scripture. They cannot rightly claim, therefore, to believe in the one

true God. When Jesus says, "Thou shalt love the Lord thy God with all thy heart, and with all thy soul, and with all thy mind" (Matthew 22:37, chapter 9), He means that to love God with any less than "all" is to not love Him. Likewise, to believe in less than every word of His Word is to not believe His Word and, therefore, to not truly believe in Him. Where believing in the Bible is concerned, it's all or nothing.

When people of my generation talk with one another about the things we see going on in contemporary parenting, an oft-heard phrase is "lost their way." It is obvious to nearly all of us Boomers that many of today's parents possess no coherent sense of direction. They're wandering aimlessly. That wandering has been intensifying since the early 1970s when the snowball of postmodern psychological parenting began rolling downhill. It has since become a raging avalanche, a hugely destructive force in culture and growing more so all the time.

Post-1960s parenting is wrong and destructive because it is wholly disconnected from God's plan for humanity. Parents who are caught up in it are wandering because they lack the vision that can only be obtained from faithful adherence to the Word. They have eyes, but where their children are concerned, their eyes do not see. They lack vision, and as such, they lack wisdom, and as such, they lack understanding, and as such, they lack a clear sense of purpose, and lacking all of that, they lack confidence in what they are doing. They lack confidence in what they are doing because genuine confidence—the unassailable sense that one is "on track"—is only possible through Christ.

The symptoms of not being on the right track, of lacking confidence of purpose in the rearing of a child, include instructions phrased as questions (e.g., "How about holding my hand as we walk across the street, okay?"), frequent requests for a child's input in making family decisions ("Where would you like to go on vacation, sweetie?"), capitulating to a child's emotional reactions, feeling obligated to explain oneself to a child, frequent parent-child arguments, frequent apologies to a child, and frequent complaints that a child is exhausting. A mother once told me, "Had I known beforehand how difficult it is to raise a child, I would never have had one." How utterly sad. Unfortunately, that mother spoke for many women. When I ask an all-female audience, "Raise your hand if raising children is the hardest thing you've ever done," it is rare to see a woman without a hand in the air. They laugh, but the implications are hardly funny. Then I ask, "Keep your hand up if you think your grandmother—who may have raised three times the number of kids you are raising—felt that raising children was the hardest thing she had ever done." All hands go down. No laughter. That's a measure of what postmodern psychological parenting has cost women, but it has also taken a toll on marriages, children, families, schools, communities, and culture.

Raising children according to psychological theory has come at huge cost to all concerned because the theory in question is incompatible with God's child-rearing plan. Postmodern psychological parenting is labor-intensive, stressful, anxiety-producing, and strips parents of confidence in what they are doing. It is plain wrong. There is not even one small thing right about it. God's plan for the raising of children is everything postmodern psychological parenting is not.

God's child-rearing design, by contrast, is relatively effortless (not to say there will be no difficult moments), stress-free (not to say there will be no stress at all, ever), and instills a sense of purpose and confidence. God's plan is a vision. It opens one's eyes. It is done primarily from the heart, not the head. It is non-intellectual. It does not strain the brain. There is nothing, not one small thing, wrong about it (not to say things will never go wrong).

Are you ready to stop drinking the postmodern parenting Kool-Aid and become refreshed with God's living water?

FOR PERSONAL PONDERING AND GROUP DISCUSSION

1. Do you possess a child-rearing vision? If so, define it in three sentences or less. If not, formulate one, using three sentences or less.
2. If to this point your child-rearing has lacked biblical vision, what have been the consequences to yourself, your marriage, and your children?
3. What are the problems that are likely to result from a vision that essentially reads "I want my kids to be happy and successful?"

35
IDOLATRY STRIKES DEEP

They exchanged the truth of God for a lie, and worshiped and served created things rather than the Creator, who is forever worthy of praise! Amen.

—Romans 1:25 (BSB)

Ye shall make you no idols nor graven image ... to bow down unto it: for I am the Lord your God.

—Leviticus 26:1 (KJV)

Wake up, and strengthen the things that remain, which were about to die; for I have not found your deeds completed in the sight of My God.

—Revelation 3:2 (NASB)

Idolatry is an insidious thing. It creeps into one's life while one is distracted and not, therefore, paying attention. Slowly but surely, the idol occupies more and more space until it has all but eclipsed the "things that remain"—in this case, things of lasting and vital importance. Idolatry clouds one's vision. It causes people with eyes to be blind and people with ears to be deaf.

Shortly after dedicating my life and work to the Lordship of Christ Jesus, I was in my car when one of my all-time favorite songs came on the radio: the sublime "Here Comes the Sun," written and sung by George Harrison of the Beatles. Prior to that moment, I had heard the song as a celebration of the end of a dreary English winter, when the sun finally pokes through the seemingly endless gloom and the earth once again bursts with light and life. This time, however, my brain substituted "Son" for "sun" and I heard it as if for the first time as a song of praise—a modern-day psalm—to Christ. (I am told I cannot reproduce the lyrics as I would like, so the reader will simply have to Google them.)

Like the thick grey clouds of winter in the song, the idols we create in our lives hide the Son from us. Idols are jealous things. The more we feed them with worship, the more petulant and demanding they become.

While my wife and I were waiting to board a plane in San Diego in January of 2019, a loud ado broke out at the gate next to ours. We looked up to see a little girl of maybe five shrieking and screaming at her parents who were trying, vainly, to calm her down. Then, much to our shock, the child began pummeling her father with her fists as her shrieking amped up. He reacted by asking her if she needed a safe space. Willie and I looked at one another, rolled our eyes, and went back to reading our books. That was not the first time we had witnessed a scene of that sort. There is something about airports, I have concluded, that sets the stage for them.

Later, Willie and I commented to one another that during our child-hoods we never, and I mean *never ever* saw a young child—a child of any age, for that matter—screaming at and hitting their parents. Today, what was non-existent two to three generations ago is so familiar that when it happens, people hardly pause to notice. The children in question are living examples of the consequences of making idols of children. The additional problem—as with the parents of the little girl in the above anecdote—is that when a child-idol begins demanding its due, its idol-makers usually give it the sacrifice it demands, the result being that the idol grows ever more jealous and demanding. It is significant to note that the little girl's father took her by the hand and headed for a store to purchase her something appeasing.

The only solution to idolatry is to put things in their proper order—to, as John put it, "strengthen the things that remain." Child-idols do not "remain." They come and they go, but not before they have inflicted great pain on others, including their worshippers. Child idol-hood also inflicts great damage on the children it infects, the most common forms of which are severe, even life-threatening episodes of anxiety and depression when they reach their teen years. These are the teens who end up in psychiatric treatment centers, in perpetual therapy, or taking dangerous psychiatric drugs.

Like the little girl in the airport that day in 2019, child-idols are not happy unless they are getting what they want. Unfortunately, as a person ages, it is inevitable that he gets less and less of what he wants. As adults, very few ex-child-idols can maintain their childhood standards of living, which means they become more and more unhappy as time goes on.

In that airport on that day, one was inclined to feel sorry for the little girl's parents, but the ultimate price of their idol-making will be paid by her, not them.

FOR PERSONAL PONDERING AND GROUP DISCUSSION

1. Are you guilty of having made an idol of your child or children? If yes, how so?
2. If yes to the above question, what are you doing to perpetuate that idolatry?
3. What steps can you begin taking to reduce your child's status in the family, to put her in proper perspective and help her put herself in proper perspective?

36

CHILD LABOR IS STILL LEGAL!

Remember the sabbath day, to keep it holy.
Six days shalt thou labor, and do all thy work:
But the seventh day is the sabbath of the Lord thy God: in it
thou shalt not do any work, thou, nor thy son, nor thy daughter,
thy manservant, nor thy maidservant, nor thy cattle, nor thy
stranger that is within thy gates.

—Exodus 20:8–10 (KJV)

Did you get that? Most people do not, so you are not alone if you think
the Fourth Commandment only says that the sabbath, the seventh day,
should be a day of rest. Check out verse 9, where it says that one should
labor for six days and *then* take a day of rest. Are you getting it now?
God is commanding not only a day of rest, but also six days of work!
They are a package!

The central theme of the story of creation in Genesis 1 is not that
God took a day of rest. It is that in six days God created the universe,
including the stars, sun, moon, Earth, animals, plants, and the male
and female from whom would come all mankind. During 86 percent
of week one, the week of creation, God performed labor! As his imagers,
we are to conform our lives to that model. The work God performed

was, in His own words, "good." God wants us to experience the sense of meaning and purpose that arises from doing a *good* job. The seventh day is set aside for rest and worship, but the preceding six days are for making oneself useful.

Work is a noble thing. It confers dignity and self-respect. Thus does a working person develop respect for others who perform labor. Along with love of God, respect for others—love of neighbor—forms the nucleus of a prosocial, godly character. Without respect for others, there is no charity, good manners, compassion, service, generosity, or anything else that comprises a sense of social responsibility. It is accurate to say, metaphorically, that work makes the world go 'round.

Notice that God clearly means for the Fourth Commandment to apply to children. As do their parents, they are to work for six days and then observe the sabbath. When God dictated the law to Moses, children were educated at home. There is no mention in the entire Bible of children waking up, getting dressed, eating breakfast, putting on their backpacks, and then skipping merrily off to school. In fact, the Bible says that a child's education is primarily the responsibility of his parents (see Deut. 6:6–7, chapter 7). One may correctly conclude, therefore, that by including children in the Fourth Commandment, God means children should begin performing meaningful labor from as early in their lives as they are capable. In most cases, that would be between the second and third birthdays. It should go without saying that the earlier children form the habit of contributing work—chores—to the daily operation and maintenance of their families, the stronger the habit will become. In the long run, good work habits benefit the children who develop them even more than they benefit their parents and siblings.

Chores—family responsibilities—define a child's role within his family. Without chores, an otherwise capable child is doing nothing but consuming food and other valuable resources. A child with no family responsibilities has no clearly defined function or purpose. He is on an entitlement program. He is on the receiving end of lots of stuff but contributes nothing. Put bluntly, he's a freeloader, on the dole, a slacker, a sponge. Mind you, he is not to blame for being a freeloader, etc. He has no responsibilities because his parents are shirking theirs. Tragically, in the long run, he will suffer much, much more than will they because just as work becomes a stronger and stronger habit over time, so does being a freeloader. A "muscle" not used becomes weaker and weaker to the point where it simply goes into a coma from which it may never fully wake if it ever wakes at all.

When people in my generation were children, nearly all of us had chores. We were not paid for doing these chores any more than our mothers were paid for cooking family meals or our fathers were paid for mowing lawns. We did our chores because chores made the family go 'round. Our chores came before going outside to play. They most definitely came before watching television (if, that is, one's parents even had a television back then). Chores even came before homework. If you were doing your homework and your parents noticed that you had not done one of your chores, they made you stop and get with the program. One's chores, furthermore, had to be done right or done over.

By the way, none of us relished doing chores. Not until adulthood will a child fully appreciate the value of toil done not for immediate personal gain but in the service of others—further proof that children, left to their own devices, would never truly grow up. (There is a pun in the previous sentence. Did you see it?)

FOR PERSONAL PONDERING AND GROUP DISCUSSION

1. Have you allowed—with the best of intentions, of course—your children to be slackers? What are the symptoms of their slacker-hoods?
2. If your answer to the first question is yes, what have been the consequences to their behavior, character, values, and general attitude of being allowed to keep the sabbath seven days a week?
3. What household responsibilities could your kids take over today? Make a list. Train them. Make the hand-off! (For where and how to begin, see the chapter on chores in my book *A Family of Value*.)

37

BE THE TRUTH AND PARENT ON

A soft answer turns away wrath, but a harsh word stirs up anger.
—Proverbs 15:1 (ESV)

In his letter to the Christian community at Ephesus, Paul advises parents to bring up their children in the "nurture and admonition of the Lord" lest they provoke them to *wrath*—the word used in the King James Version (6:4). Paul, very well acquainted with Hebrew Scripture (what Christians refer to as the "Old Testament"), might have been thinking in terms of this verse from Proverbs. Whether or not King Solomon was thinking in terms of parents and children, it certainly applies.

"I lose my temper with my kids on a daily basis, it seems," a mother tells me. Complaints along that line are common to parents who request my advice. A significant number of today's parents seem to live on the edge of near-constant frustration, a condition that expresses itself in frequent explosions of pique . These outbursts are often followed by tsunamis of guilt, followed by various forms of parental penance—apologies and indulgences being the most prominent examples. At that point, their parenting stress begins to build anew and around and around they go on a parenting merry-go-round. "My kids don't respect me" is another frequent complaint from today's parents. Their kids demand various entitlements, throw tantrums when they don't get their way, call them various epithets, and the like. And again, the merry-go-round begins to revolve.

Something has changed since I was a child, and dramatically so. I did not scream and yell at my parents, and I didn't know of any child who did. But then, my parents did not scream and yell at me either. They simply let me know, calmly and straightforwardly, their expectations and my boundaries. They let "yes" be "yes" and "no" be "no" (Matt. 5:37, chapter 14), and their sole explanation for any instruction or decision was "Because I said so."

When my wife and I became parents in 1969, the old ways, including "Because I said so," were beginning to fall out of favor. The new experts said children deserved explanations; that they needed to know the reasons behind their parents' rules and decisions. And when children didn't like their parents' rules and decisions, the new experts said parents should take pains to negotiate win–win outcomes. The problem, of course, is that children do not comprehend win–win. That is a sophisticated concept, one that's way above children's heads. Children comprehend win–lose. So, as parents try to reach compromise, kids try just as hard to get their way. The popular joke is that trying to compromise with a child is akin to negotiating with a terrorist. That isn't far from the truth, in fact. Children lean toward being irrational, self-centered, and largely driven by emotion. "We can't afford it" means nothing to them. "You don't need that" is gibberish because in their thinking, want and need are synonymous.

Parents who tell me that their children cannot take no for an answer are parents who can't say no and mean it. Said parents are not describing child problems; they are describing problems of their own! Unlike parents of the 1950s and before, many of today's parents avoid saying no. Instead, they hem and haw. Meanwhile, their children, sensing weakness, escalate their demands. Ultimately, said parents either give in or scream or both. Adding fuel to the fire, it is generally the case that if parents scream, children become sullen and angry. Maybe they scream back or they just hide in their rooms until their parents come seeking absolution for their parenting sins. So goes the merry-go-round. When does it end? Sometimes not until the child in question leaves home.

Mind you, "a soft answer" does not necessarily mean the answer a child is seeking. And it does not mean the answer must be given in a pleasing way. "No," simply put, qualifies. "Because I said so," simply put, qualifies. "I'm not going to waste my time or yours talking about this because nothing is going to change," simply stated, qualifies. "What is it about 'no' that you don't understand?" qualifies.

Keep in mind that because children are emotionally driven and self-centered, even a soft answer can stir up a child's anger. In other words, the mere fact that a parent gives a soft answer does not eliminate the possibility that the child in question will react with an emotional outburst of some sort. A child's reaction, no matter how extreme, does not automatically disqualify the parent's answer. As is the case here, many Proverbs state *principles,* not guarantees. Furthermore, yelling and screaming on the part of a child is never justified, no matter how "un-soft" his parent's speech. My default advice to parents who tell me they lose their cool on a regular basis: "You need to learn how to be mean." After a pause for effect, I clarify: "I don't mean you should learn to be more threatening or ugly or demeaning. To a child, a parent is mean when the child discovers the parent *means* what he or she says."

Be truth in your kids' lives. Stop hemming and hawing. Tell it like it is. Let your "yes" be simply "yes" and your "no" be simply "no." Say what you mean and mean what you say. Learn the art of being mean. That is how you stop screaming.

FOR PERSONAL PONDERING AND GROUP DISCUSSION

1. Do your kids have difficulty accepting "no" for an answer? If you are willing to take full responsibility for the problem, what can you do to correct that situation?

2. Do you tend to explain yourself to your kids? What have been the consequences of your attempts to reason with them?

3. What specific things can you begin doing today to become soft-spoken *truth* in your children's lives?

38

A CONSTANT LEANING POST

Trust in the Lord with all your heart, and do not lean on your own understanding. In all your ways acknowledge Him, and He will make straight your paths.

—*Proverbs 3:5–6*

The sufficiency of Scripture in all human endeavors is a difficult thing for the modern mind to fully grasp, especially if said mind belongs to a person living in a high-tech culture that believes in the ability of experts to solve any problem of living. And so, paradoxes abound. Take, for example, Christians who say they believe the Bible is the truth, the whole truth, and nothing but the truth, and yet also believe that to know how to correctly raise a child, they would do best to consult the writings of people who, like me, have capital letters after their names.

In this regard, the typical American Christian parent is no different from the typical American non-Christian parent. In the raising of their children, they both depend on the understandings of parenting experts. They are probably reading many of the same books, most of which were written by mental health professionals who have never opened a Bible and don't even believe in God. Even some Christian parenting pundits rely on sources other than Scripture! They too would agree that God's

Word is sufficient, yet they draw upon psychological theories that are antithetical to a biblical worldview.

A very well-known Christian parenting expert, for example, once told me that parents should help children develop self-esteem. As he explained himself, I began reviewing in my mind those Bible verses that specifically warn against having a high opinion of oneself or one's accomplishments. Jesus could not have been more explicit on this subject when He blessed the meek and poor in spirit and warned that "those who exalt themselves will be humbled" (Matthew 23:12, chapter 18). How a well-known and highly respected Christian parenting figure comes to believe children should esteem themselves is beyond me.

A man's understandings—those he arrives at without working knowledge of the Word—are bound to lead him astray. When the man in question is a public figure, his understandings are bound to lead others astray. Today's parents do not need experts telling them how to raise children any more than did their great-great-grandparents. America's first settlers believed in the sufficiency of Scripture in all things. They understood that to live a life that was pleasing to God required that one look to God and God alone for direction. The resulting Bible-based child-rearing was handed down from generation to generation until the 1960s, when American parents began taking their marching orders from people who boasted impressive academic degrees, mostly in psychology.

We have all paid a heavy price for following the experts down parenting roads never traveled. The roads in question are not "straight" by any means. They twist and turn and zig and zag and loop around themselves, taking the folks who travel them on equally bewildering journeys. How unfortunate! Children are not complex creatures. They are easy to understand, but only if one's source of understanding is the Bible. They are relatively easy to train up to adulthood, but again, only if one's primary parenting manual is the Bible. Depending on God's Word when it comes to raising a child will keep one's path straight. Sources other than the Word do nothing but make what is fundamentally simple into something perplexing and frustrating.

I don't mean to exalt myself, by any means, but applying one of the Bible verses contained herein will be of more benefit than reading the ten top-selling parenting books. Likewise, prayer is more effective than any therapy. In the final analysis, God is the only therapist one ever needs. That is why He is called "Wonderful Counselor"!

FOR PERSONAL PONDERING AND GROUP DISCUSSION

1. What do you think the consequences would be to you and your children if you never again consumed parenting information and advice from professional sources?
2. What do you think the consequences would be to you and your children if you began using the Word as your one and only source of parenting guidance?
3. In consideration of your answers to the first two questions, what do you intend to do from here on?

39
A SHIELD AND REFUGE FOR THESE TIMES

As for God, his way is perfect:
The Lord's word is flawless;
He shields all who take refuge in him.

—2 Samuel 22:31

This scripture is part of a song of praise and thanksgiving David composed following the defeat of the armies of King Saul and the Philistines. The struggle between King Saul and David represented the escalating tension between creeping secularization—embodied in a monarch consumed with jealousy, greed, and self-love—and Israel's original purpose as God's chosen. At issue was not only the question of who would rule her but also her very reason for existence.

As was the case in Israel around 1000 BC, twenty-first-century America is a battlefield upon which a war over her future rages, a war that pits those who would preserve the biblical values of her founding against the insidious forces of secularism. At issue are the definitions of marriage and family, the sanctity of life, the definitions of male and female, and the God-given right of parents to control the raising and education of their children. In the final analysis, however, the contemporary culture war is all about the future of the family. It should be obvious to any perceptive observer that the primary objective of those on the secular left is to destroy the traditional nuclear family—to take what God created and remake it in their own warped image.

To a student of history, that should not come as a surprise. Karl Marx (1818–1883), the philosophical "father" of socialism and communism, wrote that for the social and political utopia he described in *The Communist Manifesto* (1848) to become a reality, the traditional family had to be destroyed. Accomplishing that required two things: upending traditional understandings of marriage and redirecting the loyalty of children from their parents to the state. Marx's modern-day heirs are consumed by a passion to see his ideas not simply accepted but become law of the land, both of which are now happening before our very eyes. To cite a recent example: To folks who raised children prior to the cultural revolution of the 1960s, the idea that the Supreme Court of the United States of America would legalize marriage between two men or two women would have been beyond absurd, the stuff of off-color jokes. Yet, on June 26, 2015, that is exactly what happened.

God created marriage. Man cannot make it into something other than what God intended. But taking God out of the equation for the moment, the historical purpose of marriage was to sanction sexual relations between a man and woman and legitimate the offspring of such unions. It is impossible for two men or two women to engage in authentic sexual intercourse, and it is impossible for two men or two women to produce a child. Therefore, that 2015 Supreme Court ruling legalized an impossibility. Nonetheless, that which is impossible is now law of the land.

In America's state-run schools, young children are encouraged to report their parents if they spank or enforce any discipline they, children, consider inappropriate. School personnel, in turn, make reports to government agencies who investigate the reports of the children in question with pre-existing bias.

The United Nations Convention on the Rights of the Child, a set of principles agreed to by nearly every nation in the world (except, as of 2021, the USA), entitles children in ways that effectively demote parents to mere caretakers acting on behalf of the state. The entitlements in question include "freedom of association" and freedom to access any media of their choice, "regardless of boundaries." As was the case in the Soviet Union and is still the case in communist countries like Cuba, children are encouraged, increasingly, to see the government, the state, as their personal savior, their grantor and protector of privilege. Again, what the reader's great-grandparents would have regarded as nothing short of irrational has become (or is threatening to become) law.

The family is under attack from less obvious sources as well—the out-sized influence of extracurricular child and youth sports programs, for example. For many families, participation in these activities often supersedes all else, such as church attendance, family meals, and more valid and enduringly valuable forms of family fun like the old-fashioned picnic.

The mainstream media is clearly anti-family. In 2015, a highly popular television sit-com portrayed two men raising a little girl. Even though homosexuals make up less than 5 percent of the population, the cast of nearly every television show includes a homosexual couple. Only Satan can make people believe that down is up, wrong is right, and heart-breaking is hilarious.

In the 1990s, I predicted that pedophilia would be the next taboo the secular left would attempt to demolish. Since then, several Hollywood movies have portrayed pedophiles sympathetically, and even several Hollywood insiders have warned the public of exactly what I predicted. Pedophiles are organizing into societies like the North American Man-Boy Love Association (NAMBLA) and employing the "we can't help it" falsehood that homosexuals used, successfully, to establish a claim to victim group privilege.

In short, it is rapidly becoming clear that parents who want to raise their children according to God's plan are swimming against a cultural current that threatens to do them (and their children) great physical, mental, emotional, and spiritual harm. The question, then, becomes: what can Christian parents do to protect their families against this secular-atheist onslaught? The answer is found in this verse of David's song (repeated word-for-word in Psalm 18:30 and Proverbs 30:5). To paraphrase: *When threat and danger are all around and even closing in, the Lord God will protect (be a shield) all who place their faith (take refuge) in Him and Him alone.* What great news! There is no problem in one's life that is too big for God! In that regard, it should be obvious that politicians cannot be counted on to do what is right for the family. Even many of those who proclaim their commitment to "family values" are too conflicted, too ready to embrace compromises that take us ever closer to the brink. (Have you noticed that the secular-left never compromises on any issue?) The same is true of all-too-many of today's churches. Unfortunately, many of America's pulpits are occupied by pastors whose primary purpose is to tickle people's ears rather than speak truth.

In these troubled times, it is vital that Christian parents "circle the wagons," so to speak, and do all that is possible to protect their children and families from worldly forces that would weaken family bonds. "All that is possible" includes:

- Christian schooling or homeschooling;
- Unsubscribing to cable television and limiting video consumption to programs and movies appropriate for watching by the entire family;
- Eliminating video games and smart phones from kids' lives;
- Removing televisions from children's rooms;
- Placing all computers in the home in an easily supervised area;
- Disallowing social media accounts for children;
- Limiting participation in after-school activities such that they do not interfere with family meals or weekends, which should be reserved family activities only (trips to museums, picnics, family movie outings, family badminton tournaments, and the like);
- Family Bible study;
- Family attendance at church every Sunday; and
- Teaching children to pray by praying together, daily, as a family.

That's just for starters.

In his letter to the church in Ephesus, the apostle Paul echoed David by encouraging believers to "put on the armor of God" and "take up the shield of faith" (Eph. 6:10–17). The use of military metaphors makes clear that the believing Christian parent is truly engaged in ongoing spiritual warfare, a battle for the hearts and minds of children. A more righteous battle has never been fought.

FOR PERSONAL PONDERING AND
GROUP DISCUSSION

1. Based on your reading of this chapter, can you honestly say that you are currently doing an adequate job of equipping your children with the armor of God, thus helping them understand that in matters of spiritual warfare, He is their most reliable shield and refuge? Or have you allowed the world too much "sway" in the day-to-day life of your family?

2. If the latter, what can you begin doing today to put God at the forefront of your family, to depend on Him as a shield and refuge against a world that would use every manipulative tool at its disposal, every enticement, every entertainment, every form of propaganda, to literally co-opt your children's hearts and minds to the service of satanic secularism?

3. In what other subtle ways is the secular-left attacking the traditional family?

40

SIN IS AN EQUAL OPPORTUNITY EMPLOYER

When the woman saw that the fruit of the tree was good for food and pleasing to the eye, and also desirable for gaining wisdom, she took some and ate it. She also gave some to her husband, who was with her, and he ate it.

—Genesis 3:6

I saw her coming the proverbial mile away. Her facial expression betrayed stress, worry, and unhappiness. I was minutes away from giving a talk in Wichita, standing behind my book table, chatting with folks. She came up and stood in front of me. Our eyes met.

"I'm hoping you can help me get control of my child," she said.

"Well, I hate to disappoint you," I replied, "but I don't know how to control a child."

"But, I thought ..." she started.

"I know," I interjected. "You're hardly alone. Most parents think it's possible to control a child, but it's not."

We talked for a short while, then it was time for me to speak. As I began making my way into the auditorium, I turned to her and said, "Read Genesis, chapter 3." I hope she did.

The Bible's third chapter is, among other things, a parenting story—Western Civilization's first parenting story, in fact. In it, one finds the only perfect Parent there is or ever will be creating two children who disobey His first instruction. Right off the bat, God's first children demonstrate that, as my grandmother used to say, "Every child has a mind of his own." Understand, please, *strong-willed children* is not a subset of *all children*. Rather, all children are strong-willed. Every child brings into the world a rebellious, defiant spirit that can be controlled only by the child. A parent's first job is to discipline such that said child eventually sees the advantage of developing that self-control. Just as it is best for every one of us to submit to God's authority, it is best for a child to submit to his parents' authority. But make no mistake about it, a child submits to parental authority of his or her own free will. Furthermore, it is axiomatic that parents who try to impose their authority on their children, who try to do with their children what God has never done—force us to submit to His authority—will eventually find themselves dealing with angry rebels. In the process, these heavy-handed micromanagers—known as *authoritarian* (not to be confused with *authoritative*)—condemn themselves to an embarrassment of frustration, stress, resentment, and anger.

At the other end of the control spectrum are parents who do not control what they can and should control: to wit, their relationships with their children. These parents—they are called *permissive*—allow their children to control the parent–child relationship. They allow their children to define their roles, define how the family operates, and determine rules and responsibilities. The children in question issue never-ending demands to which their parents cater (but not without a surfeit of exasperated complaint). The parents in question thus condemn themselves to an embarrassment of frustration, stress, resentment, anger, and guilt. Note that the outcomes described for authoritarian and permissive parents differ in only one respect: *guilt*. When permissive parents get angry at their kids, they feel bad. When authoritarian parents get angry at their kids, they feel righteous.

Parents who control their relationship with their children—understanding that is the full extent of what they can control—exercise dominion in three areas:

1. *They control their children's access to them*, beginning around age two. They do not allow their children to barge into their lives at will. They are not at their children's beck-and-call. They are leaders of, not servants to, children.
2. *They control what they will and will not do for their children.* They can often be heard saying things like "Nope. You're old enough to do that for yourself" and "No, I won't buy that for you, and I really don't care that you will be the only child in the history of the world without one or that you hate me for not giving in."
3. *They control the consequences of the choices their children make.* To take but one of many possible examples, they cannot control whether their children lie (all children do, by the way), but they can and do control the consequences of lying.

On that third point, authoritative parents (again, not to be confused with authoritarian) realize they can control consequences to a large degree when their children are small and to smaller and smaller degrees as their children grow larger. As such, they maximize their control of consequences when their children are small, thus setting good disciplinary precedents that prevent, as much as possible, really, really bad stuff from happening, especially during the teen years.

The operative phrase in the previous sentence is *as much as possible*. Get it?

FOR PERSONAL PONDERING AND GROUP DISCUSSION

1. Who experiences less parenting heartache: the parent who accepts that no matter how "good" a job she does, her children are going to do bad things or the parent who denies that her children are capable of bad things? Why?
2. Have you been proactive about the possibility that your child may someday do something appalling? How does one go about mentally preparing themselves for such a possibility, and why should they?
3. Nothing interferes more with a parent's ability to respond effectively to egregious misbehavior than a knee-jerk emotional reaction. Do you tend to exhibit emotional reactions in situations of that sort involving your child? If so, what can you do to stop letting your emotions get in the way of effective discipline?

EPILOGUE
LESSONS LEARNED THE HARD WAY

There is a way that appears to be right, but in the end it leads to death.

—Proverbs 16:25

I was in graduate school in the late 1960s, when psychologists and other folks in the mental health professions began selling their progressive child-rearing advice to the American public. At the time, I was on fire for psychology. The primary formulator of humanistic psychology, Abraham Maslow, had predicted that psychology was going to save the world (yes, and believe it or not, that is exactly what he said). Behavioral psychology promised a social utopia. Freud promised humans without sexual hang-ups. Being young and gullible, I drank the Kool-Aid with a passion.

At the time, the psychological party line had it that traditional child-rearing was psychologically harmful to children. It caused them fear, psychologists maintained. A traditional approach to discipline turned children into mindless robots who could not think for themselves. One best-selling author even claimed that *all* the world's ills—war, poverty, racism, hatred, sexism, you name it—could be traced back to the psychological scars inflicted on children by parents who adhered to traditional child-rearing practices. Our forefathers and foremothers did

193

not truly love their children, claimed the new experts, but only wanted to create groveling sycophants who gratified their egos. Mind you, no prior generation had heard such a message. In effect, we Boomers were encouraged to dishonor our parents and everything they stood for, view ourselves as victims, and create soap operas out of our childhoods. As the serpent had done with Eve, the new experts promised that if we, in how we raised our kids, turned away from the lessons of our own upbringings and ate of the "tree" of their theories and advice, that we could usher in a perfect society in which everyone's mental health was without blemish and all mankind lived in a state of universal love, peace, and harmony. The new experts' promises sure sounded good.

I married Willie at age twenty in 1968 and our first child, Eric, was born in 1969. Being a student of psychology, it made perfect sense to us that our home should become a showcase for the new parenting paradigm. And so, in 1969, we began raising Eric in step with the new doctrine. In less than three years, he was running our family. When he didn't get his way, Eric threw epic tantrums that we regarded as indication of something we were doing wrong, so we would give him his way. When we tendered an instruction to him and he told us in no uncertain terms that he had no intention of obeying his underlings, we thought he was simply demonstrating a nascent genius for questioning authority and exploring the boundaries of his autonomy or some such nonsense. So, we would relent.

When he was ten, his third-grade teacher told us, with a straight face and even tone, that Eric was the worst-behaved child she had encountered in twenty years of teaching. By the standards of my chosen profession, he qualified at the time for three diagnoses: ADHD, oppositional defiant disorder (ODD), and bipolar disorder of childhood. He was a mess. His parents were a mess. Our home was in constant uproar. That same teacher told us, in January of that fateful year, that she had no intention of promoting him to the fourth grade.

"His second-grade teacher should not have promoted him," she said, "and I simply will not repeat her mistake."

Three months later, she told us that within several weeks of that January conference, Eric had become a model student. Zero misbehavior, doing his work without complaint, and doing it well. If he stayed on track, she said, she would indeed promote him, which he did, and which she did. What had happened to bring about such a sudden and amazing reversal of fortune? Through what I am convinced was God's grace, an angel of mercy in the form of a veteran third-grade teacher caused my wife and I to wake up from our utopian fantasy and begin doing precisely what the entire psychological profession maintained we should not do, under any circumstances. In a matter of weeks, we took control of our home and family, and as we did so, light began to break through. Eric became a delightful child, and our home became peaceful and orderly. I cannot overemphasize that our family's rehabilitation came about when Willie and I stopped parenting according to psychology and began parenting according to the model used by our parents.

At the time, my newspaper column—on raising children, no less!—was syndicated in some five hundred newspapers. Through the column, I began spreading the good news of traditional child-rearing. The mental health professional community responded by developing several forms of mental disturbance. Other psychologists contacted me to express their "concern" about the direction I was taking. Mental health professionals from all over the USA wrote their local papers, saying I was dangerous and predicting that parents who followed my advice would do untold psychological harm to their children. My licensing board tried to excommunicate me. When their first attempt didn't work, they tried again. When that didn't work, they tried again. In 2013 I filed a motion in federal court against the Kentucky Psychology Board for attempting to interfere with my First Amendment right to freedom of speech—they had sent me a letter demanding that I remove my column from Kentucky newspapers or face fines and even imprisonment! In 2015, a federal judge agreed with me and reprimanded the Kentucky board from the bench. Like I said, the new, improved John Rosemond provoked mental distress in people who were supposedly mental health experts .

The crazier my ersatz colleagues became, the more convinced I became that I was on the right track. Early in my career, I was an atheist, but looking back, I am convinced God was moving in my life. Around 1992, after reading several books that argued against Darwin's theory of evolution, I became convinced of the reality of God. It took me another eight years to accept that Jesus was no less than who He said He was. At that point, my life and my work took on new direction and purpose. I took up reading the Bible more than sporadically and casually, and in so doing, I began to understand the full depth of the deception my chosen profession was enabling.

Prior to becoming a believer, I thought people who claimed that God had "called" them to a certain responsibility were suffering from a combination of ignorance and delusion. It came as a shock, then, to realize that I was feeling called, insistently, to expose the falsehoods of psychology—especially falsehoods that pertained to raising children—and do what I could to help parents find their way back to understandings and practices based on God's Word. That calling has led to the writing of this book.

Satan uses human agents to confuse understandings of good and evil, truth and falsehood. He is a master at manipulating people into believing that evil is good, good is evil, truth is falsehood, and falsehood is truth. He is a master at manipulating people into believing they have made brilliant breakthroughs in human understanding, but the breakthrough ideas are usually deceptions that lead to destruction. How can I say that with such certainty? Because the Bible says there is nothing new under the sun (Eccles. 1:9). Therefore, anyone who claims to have arrived at some new understanding concerning human beings has been deceived and is deceiving others.

As I have already pointed out, the new parenting philosophy tickled the ears. It tickled mine, for sure. I fell under its sway and brought Willie along with me. As painful as that ended up being for us, it was necessary. I would not understand what I understand today and would not be doing what I am doing today if not for the fact that I became one of the deceived. To understand the deception, I had to become immersed in it, swallowed up by it, and experience the fullness of its corruption.

A pastor once told me I made it sound as if psychologists are agents of Satan. Yes, they are, but like most people who further his purposes, psychologists are not aware of their agency. They sit behind the wheel of the proverbial car but have no idea where they are headed. Take it from one who has been there, done that, an education in psychology is very seductive. It convinces one that he knows things about human beings that cannot be known without such an initiation. That false sense of knowledge leads to a false sense of power, the most potent narcotic of all. Psychologists, as a group, are some of the most intellectually arrogant people around. "I don't know" is not in their vocabulary. That described yours truly in my former life. I was incapable of admitting fault. I was my own personal savior. I thank God for that experience.

I understand the mental health profession from the perspective of an insider. It is not over-reaching to say that psychology has done far more damage than good to people, relationships, and culture. They would never admit it, but other mental health professionals know I'm on target. Every time I have invited some psychologist that I've driven crazy to debate me publicly, on his turf, at my expense—the only caveat being that I will invite the media—there has been nothing but the sound of crickets. At this point, I think they're just hoping I'll fade away. In that regard, people occasionally ask me when I'm retiring. I'm not. What I do is a mission and a ministry. I will continue to do it until I no longer make any sense (in which case I will have to be informed of my decline by a third party). In the meantime, I will do everything possible to restore God's design to the raising of children, one parent at a time.

My prayer is that this book will serve to be a beacon of light and hope to everyone who reads it. I thank God every day for the privilege He has given me. Anything God gives should be passed along. It belongs to everyone, after all.

And all of God's children say, "*Amen!*"

ABOUT THE AUTHOR

John spent his childhood in Charleston, South Carolina, and the suburbs of Chicago. He attended undergraduate and graduate school at Western Illinois University. He was awarded WIU's Distinguished Alumni Award in 1999. During his university days, John sang lead and played guitar and blues harmonica in a rock 'n' roll band that had a brush or two with notoriety. He and Willie were married as undergraduates and as of the publication of this book, have been married for fifty-three years, with two children and seven grands. They now live in New Bern, North Carolina, where they expect to spend the rest of their lives, when, that is, they are not living in their Airstream.

John's syndicated column, which he began writing in 1976, is America's longest-running syndicated column of those written continuously by one author. He's written around fifteen books on children and child-rearing, the actual count depending on whether one includes new editions. Cumulatively, his books have sold in the millions and have been translated into numerous languages. One of his books, *Making the "Terrible" Twos Terrific!*, became a best-seller in China in 2020. Ain't that the bee's knees!

John is a psychologist by training and license but refers to himself as "the anti-psychologist." As the sobriquet implies, he thinks psychology is a pseudo-science consisting of bogus theories, bogus therapies, and bogus diagnoses. He is known as a parenting expert, but his writings are based on biblical principle. He is, of course, a believer in Christ Jesus. In his spare time, which is spare, John loves spending time with Willie. He even enjoys shopping with her. He has no interest in sports, and he's still looking for another band to play with.

MORE BOOKS BY JOHN ROSEMOND

Parenting by The Book

The Well-Behaved Child: Discipline That Really Works!

The Diseasing of America's Children

Teen-Proofing

The NEW Six-Point Plan for Raising Happy, Healthy Children

Making the "Terrible" Twos Terrific

"Because I Said So!"

Grandma Was Right After All!

Helping Your Child Succeed in School

A Family of Value

Parent Power!

Toilet Training Without Tantrums

Parent-Babble